More Praise for *New Sales. Simplified.*

"*New Sales. Simplified.* is truly priceless. This is a book you don't read once; it's one you read with a highlighter and pad, taking notes on each topic. After you've read it and marked it up, you'll find yourself coming back time and time again for more ideas to help you grow your sales."
— Mark Hunter, The Sales Hunter, author of *High-Profit Selling*

"Mike Weinberg's coaching and the approach presented in *New Sales. Simplified.* have been game-changers for our firm. Our revamped sales story is getting us in front of significantly more Fortune 500 prospects, and Mike's method for conducting sales calls has changed the entire dynamic of the sales dance and helped shorten our sales cycle."
— Thomas H. Lawrence, CEO, Smartlight Subrogation

"Everyone in sales is responsible for new business development. Period. End of story. But as Mike Weinberg so clearly puts it, 'No one ever defaults to prospecting.' If you constantly struggle to generate new business, you owe it yourself to read *New Sales. Simplified.* You will learn everything you need to do to stand out from the competition, get more appointments, and close more deals. Oh, and you will have more fun doing it!"
— Kelley Robertson, CEO, The Robertson Training Group, and author of *Stop, Ask and Listen* and *The Secrets of Power Selling*

"In a time when too much of the sales literature is filled with hyperbole, tricks, and gimmicks, *New Sales. Simplified* stands out as a refreshing change. It's packed with pragmatic advice, all the result of Mike's deep experience in selling. What works in selling is sharp, disciplined execution of the basics. Every page of Mike's book reminds the reader of this and vividly demonstrates how the basics work. It's a refreshing reminder to the experienced sales professional and a critical guidebook for the new salesperson. Read it, annotate it, keep it within reach."
— Dave Brock, President, Partners in Excellence

"When you've tired of every new flavor-of-the-month sales theory and are ready to get serious about pursuing and acquiring new customers, this book is for you. Mike Weinberg tells it like it is, presents timeless sales truths, and [provides] a simple, straightforward approach to developing new business. Prepare to be entertained and energized."
— Charles H. Green, coauthor of *The Trusted Advisor,* author of *Trust-Based Selling,* and CEO of Trusted Advisor Associates

New Sales.
Simplified.

THE ESSENTIAL HANDBOOK FOR PROSPECTING
AND NEW BUSINESS DEVELOPMENT

MIKE WEINBERG

Foreword by S. Anthony Iannarino

AMACOM
AMERICAN MANAGEMENT ASSOCIATION
New York · Atlanta · Brussels · Chicago · Mexico City · San Francisco
Shanghai · Tokyo · Toronto · Washington, D.C.

Bulk discounts available. For details visit:
www.amacombooks.org/go/specialsales
Or contact special sales:
Phone: 800-250-5308
Email: specialsls@amanet.org
View all the AMACOM titles at: www.amacombooks.org

This publication is designed to provide accurate and authoritative information in regard to the subject matter covered. It is sold with the understanding that the publisher is not engaged in rendering legal, accounting, or other professional service. If legal advice or other expert assistance is required, the services of a competent professional person should be sought.

LIBRARY OF CONGRESS CATALOGING-IN-PUBLICATION DATA
Weinberg, Mike.   New sales : simplified : the essential handbook for prospecting and new business development / by Mike Weinberg ; foreword by S. Anthony Iannarino.
    p. cm.   Includes index.   ISBN 978-0-8144-3177-1 1. Selling.
2. Business planning. 3. New business enterprises. I. Title.
HF5438.25.W29295 2013
658.85—dc23

2012017452

About AMA
American Management Association (www.amanet.org) is a world leader in talent development, advancing the skills of individuals to drive business success. Our mission is to support the goals of individuals and organizations through a complete range of products and services, including classroom and virtual seminars, webcasts, webinars, podcasts, conferences, corporate and government solutions, business books, and research. AMA's approach to improving performance combines experiential learning—learning through doing—with opportunities for ongoing professional growth at every step of one's career journey.

Printing number

16 15 14 13 12 11

*Dedicated to my beautiful bride Katie,
my biggest fan, my best friend, and
still the best proof that I can sell.*

CONTENTS

Foreword by S. Anthony Iannarino   xiii

Acknowledgments   xv

Introduction   xvii

CHAPTER 1

Sales Simplified and a Dose of Blunt Truth   1

The Groundwork for a Simple Sales Model   2

Why All the Craziness and Fear About Prospecting?   5

So Many Salespeople Are Struggling: What Happened?   5

Confusion Reigns: Sales 2.0 and the Projected Death of
Prospecting   6

Where Did All the Sales Mentors Go?   8

CHAPTER 2

**The "Not-So-Sweet 16" Reasons Salespeople Fail at New Business
Development**   11

They Haven't Had To or Don't Know How   12

They Are Always Waiting (on the Company)   13

They Are "Prisoners of Hope"   14

They Can't "Tell the Story"   14

They Have Awful Target Account Selection and a Lack of
Focus   15

They Are "Late to the Party"   16

They Have a Negative Attitude and Pessimistic Outlook   17

They Are Guilty of a Fake or Pitiful Phone Effort 17

They Are Not Likable, Don't Adapt Their Style, and Have
Low EQ 18

They Can't Conduct an Effective Sales Call 19

They Love to Babysit Their Existing Accounts 20

They Are Busy Being Good Corporate Citizens 21

They Don't Own Their Own Sales Process 22

They Don't Use and Protect Their Calendar 23

They Stopped Learning and Growing 24

Honestly, They Are Not Built for It 25

CHAPTER 3

The Company's Responsibility for Sales Success 29

Why Sales Coaching Develops into Consulting 30

Sales Follows Strategy: Mr. CEO, Please Do Your Job
So I Can Do Mine! 31

A Low View of Sales: Dumping Garbage on the Sales
Manager's Desk 32

Heavy Service Burden and the Hybrid Hunter-Farmer
Sales Role 34

Illogical and Unhelpful Compensation Plans 36

Mistrust, Micromanagement, and Treating the Sales Team
Like Children 38

CHAPTER 4

A Simple Framework for Developing New Business 43

Born Out of Failure 43

Documented Out of Necessity 46

The Simplest of Models 47

A Bold Declaration 49

CHAPTER 5
Selecting Targets: First for a Reason   51

Selecting Target Accounts Is a Rare Opportunity to Be
  Strategic   52
Your Target List Must Be Finite, Focused, Written, and
  Workable   53
Segmenting Your Existing Accounts   55
Preparing for Target Selection: The Who and Why
  Questions   57
Making the Most of Referral and Indirect Selling   59
Resources for Identifying Targets   60
Pursuing Your Dream Targets   62
Targeting Contacts Higher in the Customer Organization   63
Questions for Reflection   66

CHAPTER 6
Our Sales Weapons: What's In the Arsenal?   67

Marshaling the Weapons in Your Arsenal   68
Questions for Reflection   73

CHAPTER 7
Your Most Important Sales Weapon   75

Most Companies, Executives, and Salespeople Don't Have
  an Effective Story   76
Your Sales Story Is Not About You   77
Telling the Story Is a Lost Art: Whatever Happened to
  Puffery?   80
Differentiation and Justifying Premium Pricing   81
A Great Story Produces Confidence and Pride   82
Questions for Reflection   83

CHAPTER 8
Sharpening Your Sales Story

	85
Our Story Must Pass the "So What?" Test	86
Three Critical Building Blocks for a Compelling Story	87
Why Lead with Client Issues?	87
Drafting the Power Statement	89
A Couple of Sample Power Statements	92
The Sales Story Exercise	98
What We Can Do Now	102
The Commodity Antidote	103
Questions for Reflection	105

CHAPTER 9
Your Friend the Phone

	107
Erase the Tapes in Your Mind and Let's Start Over	108
Your Mindset Matters	109
Our Voice Tone and Approach Matters, Too	110
Script or No Script?	111
Why Are We Calling? Laser Focus on the Objective	112
Stop Overqualifying	113
Favorite Introductory Phrases for a Great Start	113
Crafting Your Telephone Mini Power Statement	116
For the Inside Rep: Build a Bridge	118
Ask for the Meeting, Ask Again, and Once More	119
Three Magic Words	120
Winning with Voice Mail	121
Questions for Reflection	123

CHAPTER 10
Mentally Preparing for the Face-to-Face Sales Call

	125
It's Your Call; You Need a Plan	125
Avoid Defaulting to the Buyer's Process	127

Bring a Pad and Pen; Please Leave the Projector at Home   128
God Gave You Two Ears and One Mouth   129
Selling from the Same Side of the Table   131
Questions for Reflection   132

CHAPTER 11
Structuring Winning Sales Calls   **133**

The Phases of a Winning Sales Call   134
Build Rapport and Identify the Buyer's Style   134
Share Your Agenda and Set Up the Call   136
Clean Up Their Issues   138
Deliver the Power Statement   139
Ask Probing Questions: Discovery   141
Sell   147
Determine Fit and Seek Out Objections   148
Define and Schedule the Next Step   149
Questions for Reflection   151

CHAPTER 12
Preventing the Buyer's Reflex Resistance to Salespeople   **153**

It's Not Your Fault, but It Is Your Problem   154
Shaping How the Customer Perceives You   156
Preventing and Minimizing the Buyer's Resistance   157
Questions for Reflection   161

CHAPTER 13
I Thought I Was Supposed to Make a Presentation   **163**

Why I Hate the Word *Presentation*   164
Redeeming the PowerPoint Presentation   170
Discovery Must Precede Presentation, So Insist on a
     Meeting   171

When the Prospect Will Not Meet with You Before the
Presentation   173

Break the Mold to Set Yourself Apart   176

CHAPTER 14
Planning and Executing the Attack   181

No One Defaults to Prospecting Mode   182

Time Blocking   183

The Math Works; Work the Math   186

Writing Your Individual Business Plan   188

Preplanning Travel: Why Southwest Airlines Is My Sales
Force One   192

A Balanced Effort Produces a Balanced Pipeline   194

Questions for Reflection   196

CHAPTER 15
Rants, Raves, and Reflections   199

Manners Matter   199

Attitude Is Contagious   200

Your Appearance and Image Send a Message   201

Go After the Giant Competitor and Play to Win   202

Winners Get in the Office Early and in the Deal Early   203

Take Real Vacations and Stay Off the Grid   205

Team Selling: Make the Most of Your Resources   206

Beware Who Is Telling You Not to Prospect   207

CHAPTER 16
New Business Development Selling Is Not Complicated   209

There Is No Magic Bullet   210

New Sales Success Results from Executing the Basics Well   211

Index   215

FOREWORD

Why do salespeople fail?

Is it because they don't have some key piece of technology? Because they need a new and painfully esoteric sales process? Or because they don't spend enough time on the Internet?

Of course not. Salespeople fail when they can't execute the fundamentals. No matter how flashy or exciting trick plays may look on the highlight reel, football is a game of blocking and tackling and advancing the ball down the field. Success in any game or arena is always about the fundamentals.

Enter, Mike Weinberg. Unlike those who would sell you the new "new" thing, Mike will tell you the truth (even though it may sting a little). Mike will help you to understand that acquiring new clients is simple, but not easy.

For more than two decades, Mike has sold, managed salespeople, coached salespeople and consulted with sales organizations. His formula for producing new business sales success will deliver results for every sales organization willing to do the work and employ his approach.

New Sales. Simplified. That's an apt title because this isn't an academic treatise on sales. It's not full of theories. It's an action-oriented guide for salespeople, sales managers, and executives. It's a field guide for any person trying to help a sales team compete and win in a competitive market.

This book will help you choose the right targets. You will learn to build a plan to pursue those targets without giving up too early. You will learn to use all of the weapons in your arsenal, particularly your sales story, to prove that you are a value creator and you deserve a place at your dream client's table. You will learn to work a plan and to execute it flawlessly. If you are a sales manager, this book will provide you with the tools you need to lead your team to success.

New Sales. Simplified. It's a book of fundamentals and timeless truths, with proven, real-world strategies that produce sales results every time they are employed. Most of all, it's a book for those with the courage to do what is necessary to win new business. And win they will!

Winning new business isn't easy. But there's no reason to make it more complicated than it has to be. This is the book I wish I had when I started in sales. Take what Mike teaches and go make a difference!

S. Anthony Iannarino
www.thesalesblog.com
Westerville, Ohio

ACKNOWLEDGMENTS

I am not ashamed to have received a lot of help, encouragement, and counsel along the way, and am thankful for the opportunity to acknowledge so many who contributed to this work.

To Bob Nirkind, my acquiring editor, who not only recruited me into the world of authorship but has been an invaluable source of guidance, wisdom, and support throughout the project. Thanks to Bob and the wonderful team at AMACOM for a great experience.

To my loving mom, wise dad, and sweet stepmom, thank you for a lifetime of cheering from the sidelines and the constant blessing of your encouragement. And an extra nod to my father for generously sharing his immeasurable sales acumen over the years. To Ed David-heiser for old-school counsel and legendary sales stories (none better than heroically chartering the two-seater plane in 1956 to save your customer's Thanksgiving turkey production), and to Bill Frakes for sharing your treasured farmhouse so this book could get written.

To David Amigo for years of friendship and trusting me not once, but twice, with your sales effort. To Rob Morton, no friend is more of a sales pro, knows me better, or provides wiser counsel. To Donnie Williams, friend, former manager, and past partner, thank you for sharing so much, blazing a trail, and believing in me. To Ron Tate for great perspective and ten years of nagging to write this book. To Mark

Peterman and Shane Johnston for your keen business insights and brotherly support. To the guys from the EO Forum, Dan Glidewell, Steve Goldenberg, Rich Ledbetter, Mike Lissner, and Paul Sinnett, I will be forever grateful for pushing me out of the nest to fly again. To Joel Lindsey, Steve Miller and Paul Stolwyk for investing in me personally and modeling lives of grace. Andy Parham, thank you for your confidence, your continued challenges to raise my game, and for your friendship.

I could not be more thankful for Eric Herrenkohl and Scott Anderson, my two trusted business coaches who've made me better and become true friends. To Anthony Iannarino, for generously sharing ideas, experience, and your large platform for my benefit, thank you.

And most importantly, to Katie and our incredible children, Corey, Haley, and Kurt, thank you for your sacrifice, patience, exhortation, and understanding as I wrote. You are the joy of my life, and I love you more than I can express.

INTRODUCTION

I love sales. My passion and specialty is new business development, and nothing energizes me more than helping salespeople improve at acquiring new customers.

By day, I provide sales and sales leadership coaching to sales teams and sales managers and sales force consulting to senior executives. By night, I have been assembling my thoughts from twenty successful years in sales in order to write the book you are holding. My practice keeps me engaged with salespeople in a wide variety of businesses and I'm increasingly concerned by a disturbing trend: It seems fewer and fewer people who make a living in sales have a working knowledge of how to prospect for new business.

There are plenty of account managers and reactive-type salespeople who get by, or even thrive, when enough business comes their way. But there is dire shortage of those who can create new opportunities through their own proactive sales effort. Many veteran salespeople are victims of their own past success and easier times, when they could make their numbers while operating in a reactive mode. Others were carried along by their company's momentum and favorable economic conditions that created strong demand for their products or services. They never *had to* go out and find business. In addition, today's younger salespeople struggle because they haven't been taught how to prospect and the basics of new business development have never been modeled for them. For both young and old, the inability to plan and execute an effective new business sales attack is painfully apparent.

New Sales. Simplified. I chose that title because I intended the book as a how-to guide for the individual salesperson or sales leader charged with acquiring new business. It's a fresh look at the fundamentals and a much-needed return to the basics. The objective is to provide a framework for a new business sales attack and to offer simple, clear, practical, and actionable ideas and techniques. I hope to demystify prospecting and the entire new business development process. Veterans will be reacquainted with forgotten timeless truths. Rookies will be introduced to a simple, straightforward approach to acquiring new accounts and new business. My goal is for you to walk away excited about hunting for new business and equipped with the usable, practical, effective tools necessary to succeed.

Chapters 1 through 3 of this book are intended to serve as a wake-up call. I set the stage by sharing part of my own sales journey and the simple approach I used to become a top-performing sales hunter in multiple organizations. We'll look at the significant challenges faced by many people working in sales today. And I will gladly offer a strong contrarian voice to the ever-growing number of false teachers loudly proclaiming that prospecting is no longer effective for acquiring new business.

I'll also shine the light of truth on salespeople and share the most common reasons many fail at new business development. My intention is to hold up a giant mirror to provide a glimpse of the attitudes, behaviors, and circumstances potentially damaging your likelihood of success. Believing that turnabout is fair play, this book also puts senior executives and companies on the hot seat to examine the ways they hinder sales success. Salespeople do not operate in a vacuum; there are often cultural and environmental issues beyond their control that severely hamper the opportunity to acquire new pieces of business.

Chapter 4 switches gears and presents the New Sales Driver—a simple framework outlining a new business development sales attack.

Sales is simple. Those who attempt to make it sound complicated are either confused themselves or trying to confuse others by creating a smokescreen to hide their lame effort and poor results. There will be nothing confusing or mysterious as we dissect an easy-to-grasp and easy-to-implement model for proactively pursuing new business.

The midsection of the book, Chapters 5 through 14, provides a roadmap and instructions covering the essential elements of the New Sales Driver model. We'll identify and select strategic target accounts that give us the best chance of winning. Then we'll invest heavily in building the arsenal of sales weapons needed to successfully carry out the attack against our chosen targets. The three weapons most worthy of attention—the sales story, proactive telephone call, and the face-to-face sales call—are all addressed in great detail beginning in Chapter 7.

Chapter 12 examines what causes buyers to throw up their defense shield, and how we can alter our approach to minimize or overcome that resistance. I will offer my strongest arguments, and even an embarrassing example, in Chapter 13, making the supreme effort to convince you that presenting is not the same thing as selling.

The best intentions, target account lists, and powerful sales weapons are useless if we never launch the attack. My biggest surprise working with sales teams is how little time is actually spent proactively selling. Chapter 14 gets down to brass tacks regarding planning and executing our sales attack. We must take back control of our calendars, stop allowing others to put work on our desks, and selfishly guard our selling time. No one defaults to prospecting mode and way too many salespeople happily find every imaginable excuse to avoid picking up the phone. No one likes to admit it, but we all know that sales is a numbers game. Good things happen when talented salespeople get in front of prospective customers. It follows that more good things happen when we get face-to-face with more prospects. We'll also take an in-depth look at business planning and time blocking, to ensure we execute a high frequency attack.

An incredible opportunity lies before you. There is an oversupply of account managers and customer-service people filling sales roles, but precious few true sales hunters that can be counted on to consistently deliver new business. You can bring tremendous value to your business, your customers, and yourself by becoming proficient at bringing in new business. I invite you to open your mind to the simple, practical ideas in this book and jump in with both feet.

CHAPTER 1

Sales Simplified and
a Dose of Blunt Truth

Sales is simple. Why everyone wants to complicate it today is what confuses me.

People and companies have needs. Those of us with sales responsibility represent businesses with potential solutions to those needs. Sometimes those people or companies with needs are already customers. There's also an entire universe of prospective customers with whom we've never done business. These "prospects" have needs, too. In sales, our incredibly important, incredibly straightforward job is to connect with these customers and prospective customers to determine if our solutions will meet their needs. The more and better we do that simple job, the more successful we will be, and the more we will sell. That's sales. Last century, last decade, last year, last week, yesterday, today, and tomorrow—that is sales.

Considering that sales is truly that simple, it sure seems as if there is a great deal of confusion and fear among individual salespeople and sales leaders, particularly when it comes to developing new business.

Let's look at a few big issues effecting sales performance today. But first, let me share part of my personal sales journey and the foundation for a simple approach to prospecting and new business development.

The Groundwork for a Simple Sales Model

After a year in sales managing the Wal-Mart business for Slim-Fast, I had the opportunity to work for a fraternity brother at a small, family-held plastics manufacturer. I jumped at the chance to lead the sales effort for this company even though I truly had no idea what I was doing.

My buddy and I bought a map of United States and mounted it to a foam core board. We printed out our rudimentary sales reports and began sticking colored pins on the map to mark the location of known existing and potential customers. Too young and naive to know I was supposed to be afraid of prospecting and calling on companies that did not already buy from us, I used an industry directory to identify additional prospects and assigned a unique color pin to them as well. Based on what I could learn about our customers from studying the sales reports and speaking with the plant manager, I put together a sales plan to go out and attack the market.

It was 1993. I had a midsize company car, a legal pad, some manila folders, and a calling card for pay phones. No Internet, no Google, no LinkedIn, no CRM, no e-mail, no mobile phone, and no fear.

The business was tough. We were tiny compared to our giant competitors. Our prices tended to be higher. Does this sound like a familiar scenario? Almost every consulting client of mine is in that situation.

It was clearly an uphill battle trying to sell components to American manufacturers in a shrinking domestic market. Undeterred, I set out to conquer the world. I drove to most Midwestern markets at least once per quarter and flew to the Southeast and California a couple times per year. I visited with every customer it made sense to see.

I sought to discover what they liked and disliked about their current situation and suppliers, and tried to position my company as a better partner that was easier to work with, more flexible, and more eager to meet their needs. I asked lots of questions, toured their facilities, and talked about improvements to our product and ways we were willing to customize our service. It didn't take long to learn that it was a lot more fun calling on business owners and senior executives than purchasing agents, but that's a topic for a later chapter.

When planning sales trips to see current customers, I dedicated time to call and visit with prospects (that's how we get the scary word *prospecting*). When one of those prospects would agree to see me, I'd conduct the sales call in an almost identical manner as my customer meetings. I wanted to be perceived as someone who could bring value and help solve business issues, not just another salesman pushing a similar product or offering a lower price—especially since my price was generally higher!

After a couple of years of successfully growing sales by picking off business from competitors, we turned our attention to new markets. We identified an industry that appeared commercially viable for our extruded plastic components and set our now "finely tuned" new business development engine in motion. I gathered industry data, subscribed to trade publications, and then attended the major trade show for our target market. I strategically selected about thirty key prospects and went to work. Telephone. Mailings. Samples. More telephone. Meetings with engineers, designers, plant managers. Before I knew it I found myself in Nogales, Mexico, testing product at a major plant. I vividly remember another trip, this time to Temecula, California, where I had worked my way in to meet with the founder and CEO of *the* industry leader. The Temecula company became a flagship account for us, and recalling the story today still makes me smile.

When it was all said and done, in three years I had about doubled the revenues of this forty-year-old business and fallen in love with the entire process of new business development sales.

Unfortunately, the succession plan at this family-owned company had turned into a soap-opera-quality family feud. My fraternity buddy was at war with his grandfather, and pretty soon my friend and I were both out the door.

The lessons from those three years were invaluable, and little did I understand then how much I had learned about selling or how in demand I would be. With opportunities at other companies to pursue, I landed at a wonderful, healthy, direct marketing company with a positive and energized sales culture. This business had grown like crazy, mostly through increased penetration of its existing customer base. During the interview process, I remember telling the super hard-charging CEO that I didn't know anything about database marketing. He said the company had plenty of experts to teach me the business, but what they most needed was a sales hunter to go out, open doors, and identify opportunities for new business. And after hearing my approach to hunting for new business and the success I had with the plastics company, he had no doubts about bringing me on board.

The CEO was proved correct in his decision to hire me. I implemented the new business development process I created on the fly in my last position. Except this time, there were no current customers assigned to me. I had to decide which target prospects to pursue and build a book of business from scratch. My sales manager and the company were incredibly supportive. As I began to experience success, they surrounded me with an excellent account management team so that I could focus on finding and closing new business. I learned what business issues and hot-button topics would earn an initial meeting with prospects and dedicated blocks of time to proactively call my strategically selected targets. It's safe to say I out-called my peers by a factor of at least three to one as I worked to get in front of every major prospect on my list.

(Southwest Airlines became my friend, and I viewed its planes as my personal Sales Force One.) It turned into an eighteen-year friendship and, to this day, I consider the airline one of the most valuable resources for my business and encourage clients to take advantage of

Southwest's sales-friendly policies and pricing. It is interesting how many sales road warriors view Southwest as an essential component of their attack plan.

In my third year with the direct marketing company, I had become the top-performing salesperson out of a team of fifteen, set company records for monthly and annual sales, and earned four times what I did at the little plastics company. Life was good. I picked up my first German car and we moved to a beautiful home in a more desirable location.

Why All the Craziness and Fear About Prospecting?

If sales really is that simple, why all the craziness? Why are there so many new theories, new books, new methodologies? Why are there so few A-players on sales teams? Why are so many companies and individual salespeople not achieving their sales goals—particularly their new business development goals? Why does the mention of the word *prospecting* cause even veteran salespeople to freak out or hide?

In the next chapter we'll tackle the most common reasons that salespeople fail at new business development. But beyond our own individual attitudes and behaviors, there are a few macro issues plaguing the sales profession today.

So Many Salespeople Are Struggling: What Happened?

Having spent the past decade leading and consulting sales teams, I've come to the painful conclusion that salespeople are ill-equipped to successfully attack the marketplace for new business. That's a big statement, but here's why I believe it is true for the vast majority of the current generation of sales professionals: *Most people employed in sales positions today have never truly had to "hunt" for new accounts or new business.*

Why? Because big chunks of their sales careers to date have been during long seasons of economic prosperity. Most of the 1990s and the period from 2002 through 2007 were boom times. There was incredible demand for what many of us were selling. Salespeople could get away with being passive or reactive and still deliver the numbers. In many industries, as long as you took care of your current customers you'd thrive. Highly relational salespeople did great when the business was coming to them.

Unfortunately, times and economies change. The stock market's Internet bubble burst in early 2000. A year and a half later we endured the tragedy of 9/11. Business slowed, sales stalled, and many companies were in a tailspin. I started my first stint as a sales consultant in 2002. It turned out to be great timing because there was widespread pain and confusion throughout sales organizations. Salespeople making fantastic livings just years earlier were completely lost. Many, victims of their past success as reactive account managers, had no clue how to proactively find and open up new relationships.

In 2007, air began to leak from the real estate-driven economic bubble, and the financial meltdown of 2008 practically ground all commerce to a halt. It's been a challenging few years and we're still not sure how the story of what is now known as the "Great Recession" will end. But this much is certain: Many people in sales are struggling as inbound demand for their services has declined, and those without a reliable process to develop new business are in a world of hurt.

Confusion Reigns: Sales 2.0 and the Projected Death of Prospecting

Further complicating matters are a myriad of popular new theories about prospecting that cloud the minds of salespeople young and old. There's a myth being perpetrated today proclaiming that the *old methods* don't work anymore. Many in what's called the Sales 2.0 movement harshly declare that proactive targeting and prospecting for new business is dead. These so-called experts proclaim that cold-calling is ineffective and pursuing prospects that aren't coming to you is a waste of time.

These false pronouncements are having a severe negative impact on sales performance. It's difficult enough to get salespeople who buy in to the value of prospecting to actually block time on their calendars to do it. No one defaults to prospecting mode. No one. And most of us are masters at finding other "urgent" responsibilities to fill our days. Now we have these supposed Sales 2.0 gurus reinforcing the nonactivity and failure of today's underperformers. "Don't waste your time cold-calling. That doesn't work." Or, even better, "Buyers will approach you when they're ready. It is fruitless to engage with prospects that are not coming to you."

This line of reasoning is almost analogous to giving a sugar addict trying to get in shape a king-size candy bar. It's exactly what the passive-reactive salesperson wants to hear. Forget all that stuff about working out and eating lean proteins, good fats, and tons of veggies. You go right ahead and eat the same crap you always have and don't worry about exercise. The rules of nature have changed! You can get yourself healthy simply by following health experts on Twitter and blogging about your desire to be fit.

Over the top? Am I being a little extreme to make a point? Maybe. Listen, the last thing I want struggling salespeople to hear is that they have permission to be less proactive. As I often say, "Sales is a verb." The dictionary would argue otherwise, but experience shows that the most successful new business salespeople tend to be the most active salespeople. Good things happen when a talented salesperson with a potential solution gets in front of a prospective customer who looks and smells a lot like your other customers.

Has the world changed? Yes. Has the Internet dramatically shifted the balance of power in terms of "information flow" during the sales process? Absolutely. Can social media be incredibly effective for building community, creating a following, and driving inbound inquires? It sure can.

I'm as big a fan as anyone of new media. I connect with mentors, peers, prospects, and like-minded competitors online almost every day. I love Twitter. I have a mentor who has been like a big brother to me. We "met" on Twitter, I read his blog religiously, and we speak by phone monthly. A handful of my clients found me through social media. Funny enough, the very fact that this book is being published by AMACOM is because its wonderful acquisitions editor discovered my blog and pursued a relationship with me. So, yes, the world has changed and there are many great new vehicles to connect with potential customers and build relationships. Having said that, we must be vigilant to protect ourselves from the deceptive voices preaching deadly advice that many people in sales want to hear. Technology and new media are a great supplement to, not a replacement for, our prospecting efforts. Let's embrace the new without discarding the old. We aren't going to achieve our fitness goals by solely relying on social media, and neither will we hit our new business goals.

Where Did All the Sales Mentors Go?

Let me address one more significant factor detracting from new business development success today: a severe shortage of sales mentors.

Don't confuse what I am saying. There are plenty of sales managers to go around. What we are missing are sales mentors, those wise old vets who take young pups and newbies under their tutelage and impart years of wisdom and experience to their protégé.

The job of first-line sales manager has evolved or, maybe better said, devolved, over the past decade. Your sales manager used to be the one who took great pride in making sure you knew how to sell. Radical, I know.

I've enjoyed many memorable sessions sitting down with sales peers and sharing stories about our first sales managers and their profound impact on our development into sales professionals. From how to get the best shoe shine (whether by your own hand or from the once-famous St. Louis airport shoe-shine crew in the TWA concourse), to how to efficiently pack samples in the trunk of your company car, to how to overcome tough objections, the sales manager was the fount of all knowledge.

Not so long ago, before sales managers became desk jockeys with heads buried in customer relationship management (CRM) sales activity data, many of them would willingly invest the majority of their time in the field, actually working alongside and mentoring salespeople. That is worth repeating: Sales managers would willingly work with and mentor their people, and consider it part of their responsibility to coach their teams on selling skills.

Nothing was more valuable than "windshield time" with my manager riding shotgun in my car. He would alternate between preaching sales theory to quizzing me about product knowledge or what was happening at each of my key customers. When we would pull up to an account, he always insisted I drive around the building. He would say, "You can learn a lot more about a business by watching what's going in and out of the back door than the front door." So, of course, twenty-two years later, I'm still sneaking around the back before sales calls and mentoring salespeople to do the same.

But it was when you finally parked the car that the true sales manager turned into Yoda preparing young Luke Skywalker for the sales battle: "Tell me about your last conversation with the account," my manager would say. Then he would run through the drill: "Who are we meeting with? Describe each person's behavioral style. What is important to each person attending this sales call? Why do they think we are here today? What is going on in their business that I need to know about? What is your main objective today? What is a 'win' for us walking out of here? Tell me your plan for the call. How are you going to handle introducing our new offering? What role would you like me to play? Where are we vulnerable? What is our Achilles' heel? Which competitors are involved here? Who is more entrenched? How do you like my tie? I wore it just to help you close this sale today. Don't forget your breath mints. May the force be with you."

And there were just as many questions when debriefing after the sales call, usually at a nonchain, local eating establishment (top salespeople know the best local hole-in-the-wall lunch joints): "How did you think you handled yourself? What would you do differently next time? Did you catch their reaction and the painful flinch when you asked that third probing question about the consequences of not making a change? That was brilliant, by the way. I love how you kept digging even though you had opened the wound and knew we had the perfect solution for their issue. Why do you think I jumped in at point X, and what was I trying to accomplish when I said Y and Z? Now tell me your plan for following up, and what kind of help do you need with the proposal."

Sadly, this scene, which I truly enjoy recalling and describing, is far too rare an occurrence today. There has been a real shift away from sales managers coaching and mentoring their own people. While this trend is good for my coaching business, it does not bode well for the younger or newer sales professional today. There are too many sales-people who are more proficient at entering tasks into Salesforce.com than they are at executing the basics, like telephoning a prospect to secure a meeting. Unfortunately, much of the blame rests with sales managers who are more concerned that their people keep the CRM system updated than they are with whether they can effectively sell.

CHAPTER 2

The "Not-So-Sweet 16" Reasons Salespeople Fail at New Business Development

I love what I do for a living. One of the favorite aspects of my practice is how many different salespeople I have the opportunity to know, observe, and coach.

Between my various positions as a salesperson and sales executive, and two stints in full-time coaching/consulting, I've had the privilege to observe and work closely with hundreds of salespeople across fifty companies. I've seen who is effective and who is not. I've uncovered best practices that are prevalent among top performers. I've been able to test theories in the field, tinker with technique, and see the results firsthand. Unfortunately, I've also witnessed a lot of failure—particularly when it comes to new business development sales.

I regularly see good people who excel at many aspects of selling (relationship management, customer service, problem solving, or client retention) dramatically underperform when it comes to acquiring net new business. And after years of observing so many salespeople struggle in this area, I've compiled a list of that I affectionately call the "not-so-sweet 16" reasons salespeople fail at new business development. I share these common behaviors, attitudes, and attributes as a wake-up call, not to be negative or to belittle anyone. I typically review this content as part of my kickoff with a new client. It helps level the field and gets us on the same page before tackling proper new business development philosophy and process. The truth is that everyone in sales (starting with your humble author) falls victim to some subset of these issues.

To the seasoned salesperson, I ask you to be honest with yourself as we unpack the list. Take a long look in the mirror to see which three or four of these habits may be hindering your new business success and negatively impacting your results. To the sales newbie, you may not be far enough along to yet know which of these pitfalls will trip you up, but consider this chapter as a warning and road map of potential dangers and potholes ahead. Whether we are rookies or grizzled veterans, let's put down our guards, check our pride at the door, and try not to be defensive. Transparency and honesty are healthy first steps on the path to performance improvement.

They Haven't Had To or Don't Know How

I touched on this topic in Chapter 1. A widespread reason salespeople struggle with prospecting and new business development is because they simply do not know what to do. And it isn't even their fault. Many people in sales have never been forced to find new business. Taking care of existing customers has consistently been a reliable way to grow revenue. In good times, there was plenty of demand, and as long as we met the needs of existing customers and maintained a solid relationship we picked up business and everyone was happy.

Last year I worked with several sales veterans who have been doing what they are good at (account management) for a long, long time—some as long as thirty years. Up until recently, it worked for them. Now, however, their business is significantly off, as is their income. They are scared, lost, confused, and unsure how to even begin the process of hunting for new business.

I've also spent a good deal of time with an assortment of young salespeople from various industries. They have been tasked with prospecting to acquire new business, but their biggest hurdle is that no one has shown them what to do or how to do it. "Go make calls" doesn't qualify as either sales coaching or training. Unfortunately, the lack of sales mentors is taking its toll. No one is modeling what a proper new business sales effort looks like or investing the time to show these newbies the ropes.

Beginning with Chapter 4, we'll dive into the entire new business development process and methodically review how to put together an effective new business sales attack.

They're Always Waiting (on the Company)

Salespeople fail to develop new business because they are too patient and too slow to get into action. In company after company, I see salespeople waiting—waiting on the company. I hear excuses about waiting to call prospects until the new marketing materials are ready. Waiting for the new website to launch. Even waiting for warm leads. Please.

Top performers in sales don't wait for anything or anyone. Clear marching orders, new sales materials, training? Leads, what's a lead? Nope, can't wait for any of those. The clock is a tickin' and time is a wastin'. Top performers act. In fact, they *proactively* attack target accounts even if it means getting into trouble because they're so far out in front of the support curve.

Waiting is a key ingredient in the recipe for new business failure.

They Are "Prisoners of Hope"

Being a "prisoner of hope" is a close cousin to "waiting on the company," but it happens much later in the sales cycle. I didn't invent this term. I've heard it in many places, though I am not sure where it originated. Credit is often given to Tom Reilly, a fantastic sales trainer and author of the helpful book *Value-Added Selling*.

Prisoners of hope describes salespeople who have, for the most part, stopped working the sales process and ceased pursuing new opportunities because they are so hopeful the precious few deals in their pipeline are going to close. They spend (waste) most of their time talking about, worrying about, wondering about, that good-size contract that was predicted to close last month but didn't. Instead of doing the wise and responsible thing—spreading their effort across target accounts and opportunities in various stages of the sales cycle—they lock up, becoming prisoners to deals in the pipeline that are now getting stale and starting to grow mold.

When prisoners of hope are confronted about their lack of activity and overly optimistic projections, they usually respond in a nonchalant manner. I've even heard people say with a straight face, "I'm not worried. I'll get a bluebird. A deal will fly in; I'll get lucky and make my numbers. It always works out for me." Friends, a few moldy deals, passivity, and luck are not a winning formula for developing new business.

They Can't "Tell the Story"

Salespeople fail to grab a prospect's attention because they can't "tell the story." The sales story is our single most important weapon because we use it every day, all day long. We use talking points from our story when we are on the phone and trying to entice someone to meet with us. Bits and pieces of our "story" end up in our e-mails, voice mails, and presentations.

Is there a greater sin in sales than boring your audience? We've all

14

had the experience of being "presented to" by a salesperson who bored us to tears. So often what comes out of a salesperson's mouth is self-focused. It's all about the salesperson and his great company or offering. Frankly, I'm continually disappointed by salespeople's lack of passion and power when they speak. Let's be honest. If you're not excited about what you are selling, how in the world will you get a prospect interested?

Salespeople fail to attract new customers because beyond being self-focused, they're long-winded and their message is often confusing. Many salespeople don't invest the energy to sharpen their story, but instead serve up a pitch that neither differentiates from the competition nor compels the buyer to act.

I can't say it any plainer: Salespeople consistently fail because they can't tell their story effectively. We'll cover the topic thoroughly in Chapters 7 and 8.

They Have Awful Target Account Selection and a Lack of Focus

Many salespeople fail to develop new business because they're wandering aimlessly. Too often, they're not locked in on a strategically selected, focused list of target customers or prospects.

Sometimes they fail because they don't invest the time and brain power to ensure they are calling on the right accounts. Even the best talent will have a hard time succeeding if their efforts are directed in the wrong direction. However, more common than flat-out calling on the wrong list are salespeople who don't focus on the list they have. Salespeople are famous for lack of discipline and losing focus. They attempt to call on an account (once), but don't get anywhere. Instead of sharpening their weapons and continuing to attack the same strategically selected targets, they turn and pursue a new set of prospects. This constant change of direction becomes their death knell because they never gain traction against the defined target set.

In my personal sales experience and what I've seen from other top performers, new business success usually results from a combination of perseverance, creativity, and resilience while staying laser-focused on a well-chosen, finite list of target prospects. I'll share more about the concept of selecting targets in Chapter 5.

They Are "Late to the Party"

Being late to the party may be fashionable in the social scene, but it can be deadly in new business development. This reason for failing builds off the last. Salespeople who are not proactively working a finite list of target accounts often find themselves in situations where they are late or last to an opportunity.

When we're late to the opportunity, we tend to encounter a prospect who's already shopping and searching. Some sales gurus will tell you that is exactly what you want—a well-qualified, educated, ready buyer. I couldn't disagree more. When we're late to the party, we're stuck reacting to, rather than leading, our prospects. Their initial opinions may be already formed. They've probably begun to define their evaluation process. Instead of being perceived as a value creator or problem solver, we're now selling uphill, and already being viewed only as a potential supplier or vendor (I hate that word).

The worst-case scenario is that we end up playing our competitor's already-in-progress game. Actually, the true worst-case is when we're stuck responding to a request for proposal (RFP) that our competitor helped the prospect write! That has happened to me and, believe me, it's no fun playing against a stacked deck.

Too many salespeople get overly excited when invited to submit a proposal they were not expecting. I'm not saying that it's bad to respond to a request for proposal. What I am saying is that we are in a much better position when it was our own proactive sales work that created the opportunity for us to submit a proposal. We will look at the pitfall of overqualifying prospects in Chapter 9 and examine the need to balance our sales effort against accounts in various stages of the sales cycle in the Chapter 14.

They Have a Negative Attitude and Pessimistic Outlook

This one is as commonsensical as it gets. Can you name one really successful person who has a negative outlook on life? I can't. And I know for sure I haven't seen an overly pessimistic person succeed in a sales role. If you have, please share their story with me. I'd love to meet and study the negative pessimist sales star.

Bottom line: Sales winners take full responsibility for results. They don't whine and complain. Those who underachieve at developing new business tend to have a list of solid excuses close at hand.

Lazy, complacent, excuse-making salespeople with a victim mentality lose. Period.

They Are Guilty of a Fake or Pitiful Phone Effort

Picking up the phone to call prospects tends to be a key delineator between legitimate new business salespeople and posers. True business developers know it is something they need to do, while those who fail find every reason possible not to pick up the phone.

Some people in sales fake it pretty well. They pretend to make proactive telephone calls, but don't really do it. In the name of full transparency, this is probably the one habit I most easily succumb to.

My "fake" effort emerges after I sit down during my well-intentioned time block. I make the fatal mistake of scanning a news site or two before I start making calls. Or I'll be on LinkedIn researching a prospect and then get the bug to check my Apple stock. Before I know it, I'm changing my fantasy football lineup or checking the weather for an upcoming client trip. Forty-five minutes later I still haven't started calling. And, of course, I forgot to close my e-mail, so during that time several messages came in from favorite clients and friends. Can't ignore a request from the CEO at your largest client, can you? Another forty-five minutes pass by. Before you know it, there are now only thirty minutes left in your dedicated two-hour proactive calling session. Hmm, I'm getting kind of hungry; who should I invite to lunch? And that's how we fake our phone effort. Can anyone relate?

The pitiful effort comes from salespeople who actually make their calls, but are so nervous and uncomfortable that they're completely ineffective. Lack of confidence ruins their mental state and their voice tone. They sound like, forgive the pun, they're just phoning it in, dialing away making calls so that they can say they did it. Chapter 9 will help you master the proactive telephone call to prospects.

A whole lot of salespeople fail to develop new business because they pretend to make calls, or they're really bad at it when they do.

They Are Not Likable, Don't Adapt Their Style, or Have Low EQ

Finish this statement: People buy from people they _____. Right! People buy from people they like. Sadly, there are people trying to make a living in sales that are not very likable. And honestly, that's a problem.

There are some people in sales whose quirks, weird habits, or bad breath get in the way of success. It sounds trite, but it is reality. Some of us need an honest friend to be bold and tell us the truth about how we turn people off. I once worked with an executive-level salesperson who was a disheveled mess. His clothes, his briefcase, his persona all screamed mess. He would sit at the conference table during a sales call, lean back in his chair with one arm raised above his head, and twirl the hair on the back of his head. Finally, his CEO had seen enough and said right to the guy's face, "You need to stop doing that. It is hurting you."

Another important component of likability and connecting with a prospect has to do with communication style. We are all different. Some of us move and speak fast while others are more deliberate. Some of us are loud and emotional, and those on the opposite end of the spectrum are more quiet and steady. There are driven, "get to the bottom line as fast as possible" types, and there are the analytical types who want to hear every detail and have the patience to listen.

Emotional quotient (EQ) is a measure of your emotional and social intelligence. It involves your ability to manage yourself, your emotions, your relationships, and people's perceptions of you. All of those are kind of a big deal when you're in sales. Low EQ people, no matter how smart or driven, have a hard time establishing the relationships with new contacts and therefore struggle to develop new business.

In sales, our job is to connect with the buyer. It's a hard thing to do when we only have one speed and myopically treat everyone the same, regardless of their style. I've seen some horrific disconnects on sales calls. Rapid-fire, fast-talking, passion-driven salespeople calling on reserved, data-seeking technical buyers. Ouch! Sometimes salespeople fail to develop new business simply because they lack the perception or relational skills that allow them to adapt to the style of the person they're calling. The rapport-building section in Chapter 11 offers a simple, intentional method to take the style of the buyer into account and prepare to adapt your approach during a sales call.

Again, people buy from people they like and trust. Part of our job is to ensure we are likable and trustworthy.

They Can't Conduct an Effective Sales Call

In many cases, the pinnacle of what we do is the face-to-face sales call. Much of our work in new business development is to secure that meeting with a potential customer. Because we work so hard for the meeting, we better be really effective once we get in front of that prospect. But many in sales fail because they fall flat on their face when attempting to conduct the initial face-to-face meeting.

I've personally been on approximately 2,000 sales calls in my career, about half of them as the salesperson and another thousand as the third person (sales manager or coach) on the call. I've seen some incredible artistry on superbly professional sales calls. And I've also seen sales calls blown and butchered in every imaginable way.

Most sales calls I see are not well structured. Salespeople either go in without a solid plan or they fail to share their plan (agenda) with the prospect. Neither situation is ideal, and one of two things tends to take place. Without a clearly structured plan or agenda, control usually defaults to the prospect. The buyer ends up directing the path of the conversation and it's no longer the salesperson's call, even though it was initiated by the salesperson. The other consequence of not having a well-constructed plan is that the salesperson ends up talking way too much. Imagine that. A salesperson talking too much.

Sales calls are ineffective because the salesperson often forgets the purpose of the meeting; namely, that we are there to find pain, potential problems we can solve, and opportunities we can help capture. Many salespeople regularly confuse "presenting" with "selling." They talk a disproportionate percentage of the time and don't ask enough good questions. Even when they do attempt to probe, salespeople tend not to listen to the answers! Time and time again I've seen buyers attempt to guide or provide clues to the salesperson. Usually too busy presenting to notice, the salesperson runs right by these clues. I've even seen buyers attempt to stop and redirect the salesperson toward a more relevant topic, only to have the salesperson interrupt or talk over the prospect. Really.

Chapters 10 and 11 provide a comprehensive look at structuring winning sales calls.

They Love to Babysit Their Existing Accounts

This may be the most sensitive of the 16 reasons salespeople fail at new business development. I tend to yell the loudest when sharing these thoughts, and I also seem to get the most pushback from struggling account managers who take offense at my thesis.

On the surface, my point seems almost heretical. How dare I proclaim salespeople fail because they invest too much time and energy caring for their customers? May I take a moment to point the reader back to the title of the book and the title of this chapter? I'm not saying we don't need to serve our customers. But I am emphatically saying that a majority of those in sales prefer to overserve their existing accounts at the expense of prospecting. It's New Sales where most people need the help, not managing existing relationships.

Listen, we all understand. It's easier talking with someone you know. It doesn't take a lot of proactive thought to respond to requests from an important client. The e-mail comes in and gives us something urgent to do. It makes us feel good and useful. It also helps pay the bills, especially if our compensation plan pays the same commission for a customer we acquired years ago as it does for one we just brought on board. I get it. Everyone gets it.

The issue is that the very salesperson most offended by this conversation is the same one who fails miserably when it comes to hitting the new business quota. I see many highly relational salespeople who live for their clients' affirmation. It makes them feel good to be needed. They say things like, "If I don't take care of it, who will?" Another favorite of the account-management-leaning rep is: "I sold it. I am responsible. The client trusts me." Great. The client trusts you. I appreciate the value in maintaining a high level of customer satisfaction. But it's my job to point out the opportunity cost of a salesperson spending 95 percent of the time babysitting existing customers. That sounds a lot more like a customer service role than a sales role.

They Are Busy Being Good Corporate Citizens

This reason gets me in trouble with the human resources folks and the corporate culture police. Similar to the previous reason, being a good corporate citizen seems harmless, on the surface. What could be bad about serving on the Halloween Party Committee or representing the sales team on the company's safety task force? From my perspective, a lot! There are some in sales who would rather volunteer to clean the restrooms than have to sit across from a stranger and ask a few probing questions about the person's business and face possible rejection.

There's a lot of talk about "niceness" today. People are evaluated on how nicely they play with others and what they contribute to the team. It all sounds good. But I can confidently write that it's rarely the person voted "most pleasant, selfless member of the team" who thrives at acquiring new business. Quite to the contrary, the nicest person frequently underperforms. People who have a difficult time saying "no" or delegating work to others tend to push new business development efforts to the bottom of their list.

The salesperson who likes to walk his customer's order through production, or is the one everyone else calls for help when their iPhone stops syncing with the company e-mail, is guaranteed not to be on top of the list of those bringing in the most new business. Guaranteed. Top-performing salespeople tend to be productively selfish with their time. They have no trouble abruptly ending a conversation with a time-wasting associate. When the top sales hunter finds the copy machine jammed, he doesn't open the cabinet and start reading the maze of directions. He kicks the copier door and yells for someone to get the damn thing unjammed because he has a major proposal to get out today.

Being the good corporate citizen can make you well-liked, but it's unlikely to make you more successful picking up new accounts. We will look at ensuring that selling time is your priority in Chapter 14.

They Don't Own Their Sales Process

Salespeople who don't have a clear mental picture of the "path to a sale" or can't articulate their sales process usually struggle to acquire new pieces of business. When we don't own the selling process, it's likely we end up defaulting to the buyer's process. And not surprisingly, the buyer's way can often put us in precarious situations unsuited to our advantage.

I see this play out in a number of ways where the salesperson does whatever the prospect asks. It seems like the right thing to do because the prospect is asking for it, but that doesn't make it so.

Occasionally, a prospect will invite you to come in and make a presentation. *Presentation* is one of those words that makes my skin crawl.

I will unpack that subject further, and entertain you with the most painful experience of my sales career, in Chapter 13.

When I hear salespeople talk about a "presentation," I've learned to ask a series of questions: What type of discovery work have we done? To whom are we presenting, and what do we know about them? Why are we being asked to present? Disappointingly, the response I regularly get is that the prospect has asked the sales group to present a capabilities overview and we agreed to do it. We haven't done any sales work up to this point and cannot answer the questions I asked. But for some reason, salespeople are excited to go in and get naked without knowing any of the rules. That's an example of defaulting to the buyer's process.

Another example is the buyer asking for a proposal very early in the sales process, sometimes after only an initial meeting. The salesperson, who is often evaluated by the number and dollar value of proposals issued, readily complies. I contend that proposing too early in the sales process (aka Premature Proposal Syndrome) produces a less-than-ideal proposal and puts the seller at a disadvantage. Some of the possible dangers of prematurely delivering a proposal include not having identified the buyer's criteria for making a decision, all the key players involved in the decision, and the true underlying issues driving the request for a proposal.

Whether it's presenting before doing discovery and relationship-building work, or proposing before understanding the complete picture, the outcome is the same: Not owning and following a solid sales process limits the effectiveness of our sales effort and certainly can lower our batting averages.

They Don't Use and Protect Their Calendar

It boggles the mind that with all the apps, technology, tools, and toys we have today, time management is still such a hot topic. Hasn't it been nearly thirty years since the Franklin Planner was all the rage? Four hundred dollars to carry around a forty-pound planner!

Same story, different day. As it pertains to sales and prospecting, the calendar issue is a biggie. Simply stated, most people in sales are easily and happily distracted from anything to do with pursuing new prospects. It's the rare salesperson that has a written business plan, and even rarer to find one whose business plan is dictating what goes on his calendar.

Talented salespeople who could succeed in bringing in new business often don't because they refuse to carve out time for proactive prospecting activity. I will say it again: No one defaults to prospecting mode. No one. I've yet to see a salesperson find fifteen free minutes and say, "Hey, it's great I have this time free right now. Let me grab my target list and make a few calls to see if I can connect with new contacts and schedule a couple of meetings." Never happens.

Only salespeople that dedicate blocks of time on their calendar for prospecting activity consistently succeed at acquiring new business. Chapter 14 takes an in-depth look at creating and executing a new business attack plan.

They Stopped Learning and Growing

One of my mentors says that if you're not growing, then you're dying. Looks like a good portion of today's sales force is terminally ill. Since you're reading this book, what I'm about to share does not apply to you, but I'm shocked how few salespeople see themselves as professionals and how even fewer invest in their own development. Most salespeople read absolutely nothing about sales. No books, blogs, magazines. I hear remarks such as, "Either you can sell or you can't." Or, "I've been doing this longer than some of my customers have been alive. There's nothing new I can learn about sales." Wow! Arrogance, ignorance, and underachievement are a dangerous and ugly combination.

Every week I learn something new. I follow dozens of sales gurus on Twitter and carve out a few ten-minute segments a week to read their blog posts—which are *free* and accessible 24/7 with the click of a mouse or tap on an iPad screen. Not to be dramatic, but I don't think it is a stretch to say that most people in sales could experience transformative change if they would invest an hour or two a week reading business books and articles that can help them to grow professionally. We wouldn't go to a doctor that wasn't reading medical journals to keep abreast of the latest research or get in a plane with a pilot who hasn't been to refresher training. What makes us think we can be highly effective sales professionals if we stop learning?

Prospects are busier than ever (do yourself a favor and grab Jill Konrath's incredible book *SNAP Selling: Speed up Sales and Win More Business with Today's Frazzled Customers*) and more resistant to our sales efforts than ever before. We must continually be sharpening our skills and improving at our craft. Those unwilling to invest will likely begin failing at a faster rate.

Honestly, They Are Not Built for It

This is the hardest reason to share because it's the most personal. I don't like to tell people this, but intellectual honesty and years of observation force me to: Some people are not built to succeed in a hunting-type sales role.

I've had this experience several times. I'm brought into an organization to help increase sales and find members of the sales team who struggle year after year. Perennially, they fail to make their numbers or bring in new business. Yet, they're still there, on the team, charged with a new business quota.

This may sound crazy, but some people are just too relational to make it in a new business development role. Mike, are you saying that being too good at relationships can actually hurt your sales performance? Yes, I am. Sales hunters experience conflict, risk, and rejection on a regular basis. Very often, highly relational people (including those in sales) cannot stand the conflict and tension that often exists when trying to open new doors and convince prospects to change direction, break a relationship with an existing supplier, and move their business to us. Developing new business requires pushing past resistance. Some people are not comfortable doing that. They hear one "no" and immediately say "thank you for your time" and hang up or leave. I'm sorry, but a salesperson with that makeup belongs in a service role, and management is foolish to ever think that individual is going to deliver new business.

The other behavioral style that can severely struggle in a hunting role is the highly analytical, super conscientious type. Analytical people like to have all the data and facts before acting. Many of them live to be right, and their greatest fear is being wrong or embarrassing themselves. Well, I've got news for you. New business sales can be messy. Pretty much anyone who has done it long enough has plenty of embarrassing stories of failure, mistakes, and risk—all things that make analytical types very uncomfortable. Sales is about action, and analysis-paralysis is not a quality that tends to produce new business development success.

Whenever I share this assessment with a sales team, it's pretty common for someone to approach me afterward and thank me for the blunt honesty. They have been trapped in a role that they knew didn't fit them, but were afraid to admit it. Listen, no one wants to live a miserable existence in a job that doesn't align with her natural talent.

Although this chapter has a negative tone and bears bad news, my desire is that we would all examine ourselves, our attitudes, and our behaviors. I encourage you to spend a few minutes scanning the full list at the conclusion of this chapter. Take a long look in the mirror and ask a few friends and colleagues for their opinions, too. Sometimes we have a hard time seeing ourselves accurately, but someone who knows us well and cares about our success can offer a clearer perspective.

Which of these common 16 reasons salespeople fail at new business development are hindering your success?

1. You haven't had to prospect, don't know how, or haven't seen it modeled well for you.

2. You spend too much time waiting—waiting on the company or waiting for new materials, clearer instructions, or leads.

3. You allow yourself to become a prisoner of hope to a precious few deals and stop working the process to create new opportunities.

4. You can't effectively tell the sales story.

5. You have done an awful job selecting and focusing on target accounts.

6. You are late to the party and end up playing an already-in-progress game.

7. You have become negative and pessimistic.

8. You are either faking your phone effort or could be much better on the phone.

9. You are not coming across as likable or are not adapting to your buyer's style.

10. You are not conducting effective sales calls.

11. You babysit and overserve your existing accounts.

12. You are too busy playing good corporate citizen and helping everyone else.

13. You don't own your own sales process and default to the buyer's.

14. You don't use your calendar well or protect your time.

15. You have stopped learning and growing.

16. You just aren't built for prospecting and hunting for new business.

CHAPTER 3

The Company's Responsibility
for Sales Success

In Chapter 2, we had the individual salesperson on the hot seat. Now it's time to shine the spotlight on the company and its responsibility for sales success. Let's be fair. It's not all on the shoulders of sales. There are an array of factors completely outside the control of the salesperson and the sales organization. These factors can be obstacles and impediments to executing a successful new business sales attack and are worth addressing here.

I am typically brought into a company when there is a desire to significantly increase the effectiveness of the sales organization or when the sales team is not working the way it's supposed to, particularly in the area of acquiring new pieces of business. Because I'm a sales guy at heart, I'm biased toward the salesperson. I proudly admit it. I bleed sales. First and foremost, I see situations first through the lens of a sales hunter and next through the eyes of a sales executive or consultant. That bias works in my favor as I build relationships and begin coaching salespeople. They trust me because I'm one of them.

The beauty is that because of my outside professional role, senior executives and CEOs actually listen to me (most of the time). I learned a long time ago that what sounds like whining and excuses from an employee is often considered brilliant counsel when presented by an outsider. Same thoughts coming from a different person in a different position. A prophet is not welcome in his own home? As true as ever.

Why Sales Coaching Develops into Consulting

The primary objective of my initial engagement with a company is almost always to coach the sales team, or at least certain members of the team, including the leader or manager. Nothing is more energizing to me than helping salespeople and sales leaders become more successful at acquiring new business. I address the "not-so-sweet 16" reasons I see salespeople failing and then begin coaching through the topics presented in the balance of this book. That's my passion and what I love to do.

But more often than not, an interesting metamorphosis occurs as my coaching relationship progresses with a sales team. As I continue to ask questions, spend time with members of the team individually and in group sessions, roam the hallways, and even attend sales calls, a picture emerges that's different from what was originally painted by the senior executives who engaged me. I'm not intimating that they lied to me, but I do realize after dozens of engagements that there's often more than one side to the story of why sales results are not what they should be. Not concerned with corporate politics and certainly not fearful of losing my job (ah, the freedom of not being an employee!), I dig deeper and continue to pull back the covers, often exposing some pretty serious anti-sales issues. That's when what began as a simple sales coaching assignment morphs into a full-blown consulting engagement. Most executives and CEOs who truly want to fix their sales issues welcome the intrusion and are thankful for an honest outsider who can hold up the mirror close enough for them to see why their team is not achieving the desired results. Let's examine some of the widespread issues hindering the success of sales organizations.

Sales Follows Strategy: Mr. CEO, Please Do Your Job so I Can Do Mine!

One of the non-negotiables for a sales organization to succeed in acquiring new business is *clarity*. I have yet to see an individual or a sales team have demonstrable success in the marketplace without a crystal-clear picture of their mission. Let me say it another way: Sales is supposed to follow strategy. The sales team's job is to take a clear strategy and execute it to perfection in the market. Salespeople should not be making it up as they go along. Where I'm from, it's the chief executive's job to determine and articulate the company's strategy. It's essential to be able to inform the sales team about:

- ► Our reason for existence
- ► The direction the company is headed and why it's the correct course
- ► What we sell and why we sell it
- ► Which markets to pursue and where we are positioned in those markets
- ► The competitive landscape and how we stack up against competitive offerings, and why we're better or different
- ► Why our pricing model is appropriate for the value we create in the markets we're pursuing and against the competition we're facing

The salesperson or sales organization is entitled to super clear answers for each of the previous bulleted items. Sadly, too often those answers do not come. The primary reason I walked away from my last position as head of sales was because the company could not answer those questions and it became fruitless attempting to lead the sales team through the wilderness. When that's the case, 100 percent of the sales shortfall lies at the feet of the CEO, not the head of sales, and certainly not on the sales rep. It is not the job of sales to set strategy. It's our job to execute the clear strategy provided to us. Mr. CEO, please do your job so we can do ours!

A Low View of Sales: Dumping Garbage on the Sales Manager's Desk

Some organizations are sales-driven and some are not. In my first few jobs, sales ruled the world. Slim-Fast was run by an entrepreneur who played the role of salesperson-in-chief. What sales needed, sales got. My fraternity buddy and I turned the little plastics company upside-down. We were partners in crime. I went out to the market and told him what was needed to get deals done. He had my back at the office and made sure that the customers and I were well taken care of. As director of sales, I never once felt that the company wasn't fully behind my sales effort. Then, at the direct marketing company, I began to fully understand what a sales-driven company looked like. Salespeople were close to royalty: They had better offices, more respect, rich compensation plans, and the ear of the CEO. If it ever came to a showdown between sales and operations, or sales and finance, the safe money bet on the salesperson coming out on top. It was the ideal environment for sales and produced a winning sales culture and incredible revenue growth.

I was disappointed to learn that my experience was pretty unique. Most companies have a painfully low view of sales, quite unlike the companies where I had thrived. In many organizations, the cacophony of complaints about the sales team can drive you mad. Any of these remarks sound remotely familiar?

"The salespeople use too many samples." "The sales team isn't using the materials we gave them." "The sales team is authorizing too many returns." "Your people are not attending the all-company meeting on Tuesdays." "How come he took that million-dollar client to such an expensive dinner?" "Have the salespeople do their paperwork and administrative work on weekends." "Did you see the proposal we sent out? It was awful." "The plant really screwed up this big order; grab a few salespeople to help unpack and repack these boxes; they're not doing anything anyway." "Why did he fly to Nashville when it's only a five-hour drive?" "Tell the salespeople they can ship out their own sample requests." "She tipped 18 percent and our policy clearly states that we should only tip 15 percent." "That customer is complaining that the salesperson didn't return his call within thirty-eight seconds." And so on...

Basta! Enough! For whatever reason, in too many companies salespeople are treated like the enemy and the problem. It is wrong; it doesn't help; it certainly doesn't increase sales.

Sales managers are often not treated with the respect they deserve. A few years back, I was chief sales executive for a $90 million distributor in a tough economic environment. After a year leading this forty-person sales organization, we reorganized to reduce costs in response to the severe drop in demand for our products. As part of the cost-saving measures, I agreed to insert myself as sales manager over one of our divisions. So, along with the bigger picture job, I was now also directly managing six frontline salespeople and moved my office into their location.

The president of this division was a detail-driven control freak. He was a nice man; I liked him personally. But he had a very low view of the sales function, and as a result, the company treated the sales manager's desk as the garbage dump for all problems. On my second day as sales manager, I received a call on my cell phone from an angry customer. There was some quality issue with a product, and the customer started peppering me with all kinds of technical questions. As this man went on and on, all I wondered was how in the world he got *my* cell phone number. The company had a qualified customer service group, a supply counter staffed with product experts, a product installation technical expert, and six salespeople more qualified than me to handle this customer's issue. There was no way this matter should have ended up on my desk, and it certainly didn't warrant a call to my cell phone.

Deploying my amateur private investigator skills, I uncovered the customer service rep who gave the customer my number. I asked two questions to this seasoned CSR: Can you tell me what made you think I could properly answer this man's technical questions on my second day on the job? And why in the world did you give out my cell phone number to our 248th largest client? Without blinking, she responded that all problems go to the sales manager. Not anymore, they don't, sweetheart. All problems *used to go* to the sales manager, which is why your sales team is so screwed up.

Heavy Service Burden and the Hybrid Hunter-Farmer Sales Role

I don't expect to get the Rocket Science Award for this one, but I believe it's the single largest issue detracting from new business development success. When I start digging in with a client to help assess why the company's salespeople are not acquiring new business at the desired rate, in almost every case I can make this brilliant observation: The sales team spends very little time proactively working target prospects for new business. Earth-shattering conclusion: *little effort = little results.*

Three of my current clients are frustrated their people aren't bringing in more new business. However, in all three situations, they've placed a heavy service burden on the salesperson. Each of the businesses is completely different from the others, but all three are asking their people to invest an inordinate amount of time servicing customers—quoting, taking orders, fighting fires, handling customer service issues, shepherding projects through production, etc. Again, I'm all for keeping our current customers happy and retaining them as customers. But senior leadership can't have it both ways. Don't hire me to coach your sales team to improved proficiency at new business development and then not free up their time to actually do it.

The hybrid hunter-farmer sales role is the model that dominates small and mid-size companies. I understand that there's no easy solution. If there was, we'd all be implementing it. But I want to be very clear here: This single issue is hurting new business development sales more than any other issue today.

I'm going to use hunting and fishing as metaphors to illustrate my point. First, let's talk hunting. There are very few successful sales hunters. Most organizations would agree that only 10 percent to 15 percent of their sales team could be classified as true A-player hunters that can be consistently relied on to deliver new business year after year. However, most companies would also agree that solid sales farmers, aka account managers, are in much greater supply. The problem facing most companies is very logical. They're short on acquiring new business because they're short on effective sales hunters. That follows, right? So here's my question: If we have so few good sales hunters and we're falling short of our new business acquisition goals, why do we task the few hunters we have with so much account management work? Especially when we all agree there are an abundance of account managers.

Now, let's talk fishing. Imagine we have a seafood business. We fish for giant fish like marlin and then sell fully prepared fish to our clients. We fully acknowledge that only one person out of nine on our staff is any good at catching fish. The other eight play at it and get lucky once in a while, but it's really our one star that brings in almost all our big fish. But for some reason, our business model dictates that our star catcher of big fish must do a lot of work after catching the fish. In fact, policy says he needs to bring the fish back to our office, and since he caught it, he also must clean it. After it's cleaned, he also gets to prepare it and then cook it to the liking of our guests that evening. After cooking the fish, our star proudly serves his big catch to our guests. And when dinner is over, we ask our star to bus the tables, do the dishes, and help get the kitchen cleaned up. All in all, our top producer gets to spend maybe 25 percent of his time fishing.

Okay, what's wrong with this story? Idiocy, right? Is this any different from how most mid-size sales teams operate today? We complain that we aren't catching as many fish as we would like, but our best fish catcher only gets to fish 25 percent of the time. And we ask him to do ten other tasks that others are capable and willing to do.

How dense are we? Play this out with me. What might happen if we freed up our star fisherman? What if we removed much of the burden that comes after landing the fish? Wouldn't he then be able to spend more time researching better places to fish? Instead of doing the dishes, he might have time to sharpen his fishing skills and become even more proficient than he is now. How many fish might our best guy catch if we better supported his efforts and set it up so that he spent 75 percent of the time fishing instead of 25 percent?

I understand most sales organizations are not set up to work that way. But I also understand most organizations are not achieving the new sales success they want, either. I'm tired of hearing about efficiency and legacy systems. Maybe it's time to do hard work deconstructing the model that's not working and rebuilding it with a fresh perspective.

Illogical and Unhelpful Compensation Plans

Since I'm on a streak tackling a host of sensitive topics, I might as well go for it and touch the third rail (for anyone who's not an urbanite, the third rail carries the power to the subway trains and there's enough voltage passing through it to light up a small country). Medicare is often referred to as the third rail of politics; touch it and you die. Let's talk about sales compensation.

Compensation is a sticky topic because you're dealing with people's livelihood, and everyone from the CFO to the rookie sales rep gets nervous when there's discussion about changing it. I get that, and having lived through multiple comp plan changes as an employee, I am particularly sensitive to how plan changes are perceived by the team, and even more so by top performers. Smart salespeople work the comp plan. Period. It's in the best interest of the company to make darn sure that the plan is driving the behavior we want it to drive.

I have two major pet peeves with sales compensation. The first has to do with the percentage of fixed, or base, compensation. And the second deals with treating all sales the same in terms of how they are commissioned.

In general, I've come to believe that too large a portion of total sales compensation is fixed (or base). There are entire books and consulting practices dedicated to compensation, so I won't pretend to do this conversation justice here. However, my main point is that there's not enough discrepancy between what top performers and bottom performers earn. Studies consistently show that top salespeople are motivated by competition, return on investment (or return on effort), and the opportunity to earn more money. My simple theory states that the more variable the possible results, the more variable the total compensation should be. If it's a steady business with little chance of gaining or losing business, then the plan should have less variation with a higher percentage of base compensation. However, if there are potentially wide swings in results, there should similarly be large potential swings in compensation.

Too often I see underachievers being overpaid and top producers being underpaid. Read that last sentence again and think about the consequences. I'm arguing that most compensation plans do the opposite of what we want: retain the underperformer and cause the top performer to look for work elsewhere, where her compensation will be more equitable for the results she achieves. That model is silly.

The second peeve has more to do with driving new business acquisition. In companies where salespeople maintain a book of business, very often commission is calculated based on that salesperson's total sales. It's a straightforward calculation: X sales at Y commission rate = Total commission check. My disagreement is with the fact that all sales are treated equally. From the CFO's perspective, I get it. A dollar of sales produces a certain percentage of gross profit and there is money allocated to pay the salesperson for selling expense. A dollar is a dollar is a dollar.

I would argue that when trying to acquire new accounts and influence the behavior of money-motivated salespeople, a dollar is not a dollar. If I'm fat, dumb, and happy, with a great portfolio of accounts (either given to me or acquired by me), and I'm enjoying the living that portfolio throws off, explain to me why I would not overservice those existing accounts. If my existing client base is essentially a commission annuity that will pay me the same amount every year as long as I maintain it, you can bet your ass that my first priority will be to do everything possible to keep those clients happy and buying from me. Why would I even think of taking my eye off this income stream and distract myself by going after new business—new business that takes a lot of time and energy to produce?

Again, the company says it wants its people focusing on acquiring new accounts. But just like the service burden and account management situation, the compensation plan is not set up to encourage the behavior that management says it wants. If we truly want to incentivize salespeople to pursue and close net new business, then the comp plan should communicate that loud and clear. Said less pleasantly, put your money where mouth is.

I'm a fan of plans that decrease the commission payout on existing business over time and bonus the commission for new business that is closed. Radical. *Align the pay plan with the business goals.* Make the annuity less attractive over time to encourage more hunting. And drive that point home by paying an overly generous commission in year one of new deals.

Mistrust, Micromanagement, and Treating the Sales Team like Children

Lastly, I want to address the company's responsibility for creating a culture that promotes sales success. Sales is a unique profession. My former partner at my first consulting business was a master at creating a sales culture. Donnie continually preached the importance of having a sales environment that was fun, energized, competitive, results-focused, and heart-engaging. Sales is as much about the heart as it about the head, he'd say. I knew what he meant, but couldn't fully grasp the importance of the concept because I'd only worked in positive sales cultures, including working for him before we launched our business together.

Over time I've been exposed to more and more companies with unhealthy sales cultures. I've seen controllers run wild, taking deductions from commission checks with little explanation to the salesperson. I've seen vice presidents of sales lead by fear, intimidation, and humiliation. I've seen CEOs who incorrectly believed they were sales experts tell salespeople exactly how they should approach a prospect and conduct a sales call. And most recently, at a *former* client, I witnessed the worst case of mistrust, micromanagement, and treating salespeople like children you could imagine.

I was referred to this client and had a few extensive phone conversations with the president before starting the engagement. It was a smaller company that sold very high-end products. The company had done a complete sweep of its sales organization and was practically starting over when I arrived to begin coaching a young sales manager and a fresh crop of salespeople. There were some glaring issues that emerged during my first few days on-site at the client's headquarters. Here is an excerpt from a note I sent to the president after the first month:

One of my big takeaways from the first month of this engagement is that we must create a positive sales culture at Superior, Inc. There is a general feeling of unsettledness among members of the sales team, including Terry (the sales manager)....

I also sensed an undercurrent of an anti-sales culture at the company. Lots of critique of the new sales hires' handling of customer objections, requesting samples, inability to get appointments, failure to write orders, etc...

... I think it is important to hear from an outsider that there is a cultural anti-sales feel at the company. If not changed,

this practice will prevent Superior from building the type of successful sales team it desires.

My frustration with this client and the president mounted. He treated the salespeople like they were children, not allowing them to make even inconsequential business decisions about their territories and customers. I became uncomfortable with the role I was playing. I didn't sense that I was getting my points across and began debating whether I should maintain the relationship. The president began talking about this latest round of sales "mis-hires" and the possibility of needing to replace much of the team again. I also realized that my counsel was neither sought nor followed. The president was simply using me for training the people and improving their sales process.

At the time, I had just returned from a conference where I sat under the teaching of Alan Weiss. Alan is a masterful consultant and coach to other consultants. He shared something that stuck with me and applied to my situation: If you cannot improve the client's condition, then you should stop taking the client's money. I knew he was right. I decided to fire my client and took my best shot at trying to wake up this president. My hope was he would understand that I felt strongly enough about what I believed to walk away from his business. I left him with these parting thoughts:

Sales is not accounting. It's not warehouse work. For that matter, it's not like any other job. Sales is about people connecting with other people. When sales reps walk into an account, their demeanor, their pride in the company, their energy level, their confidence, their ability to personally connect with the buyer all matter—a lot. Salespeople have to believe in their company, and they must have their hearts engaged to succeed.

But I find exactly the opposite happening at Superior. There is almost a disdain for the sales team, and you can sense the reps' negative feelings toward the company growing. This is not a recipe for sales success, and also makes sales coaching a waste. We can spend all the time we want sharpening the sales story and instructing how to conduct professional sales calls. It's meaningless if the people have no passion for their jobs…

As I shared on the first page of this note, I don't understand how a next round of hires will be any more successful unless there is significant cultural and structural change to the sales organization.

I meant that line about sales coaching being a waste if the salespeople have no passion for their jobs. It's true. You have to want it! Just as important as having a clear strategy and a logical compensation plan, companies share in the responsibility of creating an environment that promotes healthy, positive, engaged salespeople.

CHAPTER 4

A Simple Framework for Developing New Business

I had a ten-year run as a sales hunter to refine my personal new business development sales process. *Personal* is the keyword in that sentence. It never crossed my mind that one day I might be sharing this process with others, let alone writing a book on the topic. I tell my children that when you use the words "*always*" or "*never*," you probably aren't telling the truth. But in this case, I am. Never did I picture myself becoming a coach, consultant, or author.

Born Out of Failure

I left the awesome direct marketing business about nine months after it was sold to a gigantic public company. The handwriting was on the wall and it became obvious the new owners were intent on wrecking everything I loved about the place. Not wanting to miss my opportunity to get in on the tech bubble and become an Internet millionaire, I jumped on board with a web-based learning management company

43

that gave me a generous guarantee and a spreadsheet worth of phantom stock options. I was convinced this was it. A few years down the road I'd be famous for delivering more new business than anyone dreamed. The company would get acquired, we'd all be bazillionaires, and I would ride off into the sunset in my charcoal gray over burgundy leather Porsche 911.

It didn't play out quite as planned. The bubble burst, venture capital dried up, and Internet start-ups with negative cash flow fell out of vogue. But it was still a high-paying job in an entrepreneurial company with great people. We supposedly had a powerful solution and I had a framework for finding and closing new business. What could be bad? A lot.

I came to the new company with a one-page sales plan. I sketched out a dozen questions for which I needed answers to begin attacking the market. Whenever I would meet with my boss to review the questions, our conversations grew progressively more perplexing as it became clear that there were no coherent answers.

The first few questions I asked were about selecting target markets and prospects. And the first few answers basically amounted to telling me to start by calling on my family and friends. I hadn't realized I joined Northwestern Mutual to sell life insurance! By the way, I am a very happy Northwestern Mutual client and have nothing but respect for the company and its sales agents. After explaining to the partner in charge of sales (my boss) that I had reviewed my roster of relatives and friends and no one on the list was in a position to purchase an enterprise learning management system, I asked him who I should target next. Were there certain vertical industries or types of businesses more likely to need a learning management system? How about company size or geography? Without flinching, he simply said that what we had was hot, every decent size company with training content could use it, and I should have no problem finding opportunities. Right.

Not long after I started, I was assigned to work with our major channel partner. Looking back, that was probably my punishment for asking too many questions the first week on the job. This channel partner was a behemoth of an organization with more people, positions, and overhead than the federal government. But they did have deep relationships with many Fortune 500 companies and a strong training and learning offering.

I was new to selling through partners. When I asked how to proactively begin working our partner's accounts I was told to wait. *Hmmm. Wait?* See reason No. 2 in Chapter 2. Wait on what? I was told to wait for their sales force or learning experts to summon me for a meeting with one of their clients. Excuse me, *you're paying me how much to sit and wait?* You want me to sit here in this very quiet office filled with mouse clicks and whispering software developers (free soda and a foosball table) to wait for someone to invite me to a meeting? Shoot me now.

It gets better. Still perplexed about this reactive approach, I inquired what I was supposed to do when the partner scored a meeting for us with one of its clients. How do I prepare for the meeting? What type of discovery work can I do on the front end? How should I conduct the sales call alongside the partner? By this point, you can predict the frustrating answer. I was told not to worry about it. The channel partner owned the relationship, knew the client's situation, and would lead the sales call. My job was to show up, be passionate, do a presentation highlighting the magnificence of our superior system, and then conduct the "demo." I'm getting queasy just writing it! Presentation and demo. Two of my least favorite sales words in the same sentence. If you're not the patient type, feel free to jump ahead to Chapter 13 to see what took place on one of these "presentations." You'll come to hate the word, too.

Bottom line is that this little learning management system company failed. I failed. It was awkward and painful. I was one of the first people tossed off the ship to lighten the load as we were going down. In less than twelve months, I had gone from record-setting top salesperson to being fired for the first time in my life. It was one of the most valuable experiences of my career. It certainly was foundational.

I promised myself, "Never again." Never again would I let someone else dictate my sales process.

What does that story of failure have to do with this chapter on a simple framework for developing new business? Everything. I became more convinced than ever that I really did have a proven formula for acquiring new business. It took the painful lesson of being prevented from using it to realize that I might have something valuable and useful to others.

I spent a short stint at an intriguing boutique consulting firm. The firm self-destructed because of an overabundance of partner ego and a scarcity of revenue. Another valuable life lesson: **Too much ego + Too little cash = Short-lived partnership.**

But what emerged from the ashes was a thing of beauty. My friend and former sales manager Donnie was part of that little consulting practice. He'd begun doing sales consulting for a few clients. When it all blew up he came to me and asked if I'd join him in launching a sales coaching and consulting business. My immediate answer: I don't think so. Reeling from having lost my job for the second time in two years, I just wanted to get a real sales job in a real company. Give me an opportunity to sell something and I'll go out and do my thing. Three kids, a wife at home, and a fat mortgage payment required cash flow. I couldn't stomach the thought of going very long without income.

Documented Out of Necessity

Donnie could sell, and he did a number on me. "Come on, Mike. You're the best new business salesperson I've ever seen. Do this with me. I'll do my management and leadership thing, and you'll teach people how to sell, use the phone, structure calls—all that new business stuff you love. We'll have a blast." It was a good sales pitch, and since I had nothing imminent in terms of another job offer, I agreed to help get Donnie started. The business took off like the jet that was part of our logo. I jumped in with both feet, and for four years never looked back.

Very quickly, we had more clients and sales meetings to lead than we had content. I spent what seemed like a month straight working into the wee hours of the morning cranking out coaching content. For the first time, I was forced to articulate my theories about sales and a process to develop new business for someone else's consumption. What I'd done intuitively for years needed to be codified and then converted to usable material. Donnie is a gifted teacher and he was extremely helpful turning my raw content into teachable modules and lessons.

One of our very first clients was the Bank of America Premier Banking team in St. Louis, which was led by a supremely talented woman who engaged us to infuse her team with energy and coach them to proactively pursue new lines of business from clients within their portfolio. The ink on the PowerPoint was barely dry when I stood in front of that team to share the introductory module of what I now call the New Sales Driver for the first time. Considering how fresh the material and how green the facilitator, the session went swimmingly well.

The Simplest of Models

It's been ten years, fifty client engagements, and two stints as a corporate head of sales since the New Sales Driver debuted at that Bank of America meeting. It's been heavily road-tested, revised, and refined. With each tweak, it has become more and more simple.

THE NEW SALES DRIVER

A. Select *targets.*

B. Create and deploy *weapons.*

C. Plan and execute the *attack.*

It's as clear and simple as it gets. These are the three essential components for establishing a new business development sales initiative. I'm not a war hawk and know very little about military operations. If you're an ultimate pacifist, my hope is that the battle metaphor is not a stumbling block. There are many similarities between prospecting for new business and planning for war, and I've found these descriptive phrases to be exceedingly helpful when communicating this framework to salespeople and companies.

If we're committed to proactively going after new business, then we must have a clear picture of the customers we're targeting. It's challenging, to say the least, to pursue something if you do not know in which direction to head. Therefore, *selecting targets* is the first piece of the puzzle and first aspect of our new business framework. I'll offer some rules, theories, guidance, tips, and options regarding target selection in the next chapter.

When attacking targets, it really helps when we're able to *create and deploy the necessary weapons.* There's an entire arsenal of weapons available to the salesperson. Not only must we be armed, but it's critical that we become proficient firing those weapons at selected targets. Most of my coaching time and much of the balance of this book is dedicated to ensuring salespeople are armed with the essential weapons and become highly effective at using them.

Finally, we come to *planning and executing the attack.* I like to say that it's all academic unless you actually take the field. Selecting the right targets and possessing the appropriate weapons are meaningless unless we get into action. Remember: SALES IS A VERB. Planning our sales attack forces us to have discipline and to take a hard look at our calendars. We need to declare what weapons we'll be shooting at which targets, and when. And then we must do it, monitoring and measuring our activity along the way. If you recall, several of the "not-so-sweet 16" reasons salespeople fail at new business development stem from lack of execution. We'll tackle this topic in Chapter 14.

A Bold Declaration

After ten years using this framework intuitively as a frontline sales hunter, and another ten formally as a sales leader, allow me to make a bold declaration: If an individual salesperson or a company's sales team is not successfully acquiring new business, the cause of the failure can be found in one of the three components of the New Sales Driver. Said another way, if we are not closing new deals, the problem can be identified either as:

- ► Poor target selection or lack of focus on selected targets
- ► Lame sales weapons or lack of proficiency deploying weapons
- ► Inadequate planning or lack of execution of the plan

Truth be told, most sales teams struggle with more than one of these three issues.

However, there are a few critical assumptions that accompany my declaration. Yes, assuming can be dangerous, but in order to help fix a sales problem, we need be assured it's a sales problem. I guarantee that the sales problem lies in one or more of those New Sales Driver categories, assuming:

- ► The business has a clear strategy, a defined place in the market, and there is demand for its offering.
- ► The sales compensation plan is not working against the desired sales effort.
- ► The sales talent would at least qualify as "average."

Those are not outlandish assumptions. Said simply: The business knows what it is and where it is going; the pricing model makes sense based on the value delivered; the compensation plan is not incenting salespeople not to sell; and the person or people in question would rate as a B- or better.

Establishing an effective new business sales initiative is not complicated, especially when the business has a clear picture of the market it is attacking. We strategically select target accounts. We arm ourselves with the weapons required to pursue those targets and become proficient at firing those weapons. And then we plan and methodically execute the attack. New Sales. Simplified.

CHAPTER 5

Selecting Targets: First for a Reason

When charged with acquiring new business, the natural and essential first questions are: "Where is the business going to come from?" and "Who should I be pursuing?" If we are putting together a prospecting and new business development sales attack, we need to know where to go and whom to target. That's why selecting targets is the first step in the process. Quite simply, we can't prospect if we don't know who the prospects are.

Most salespeople spend the majority of their time in reactive mode responding to potential opportunities that come their way. The need for a defined list of target accounts does not register because, honestly, they are not targeting anyone. However, the proactive new business hunter requires a strategically selected list of appropriate target accounts in order to launch the attack.

Selecting Target Accounts Is a Rare Opportunity to Be Strategic

It's surprising how often senior executives or even first-line sales managers take for granted that their people are working the right accounts. Choosing our target accounts, which effectively also means choosing how we should be investing our time, is one of the few truly strategic things we do in sales. Think about it. Most of what we do every day involves executing a repetitive behavior. We work the process and work the math. Salespeople excel because they figure out how to win business and then replicate their behavior over and over. Choosing the accounts on which we'll focus our proactive energy provides a rare opportunity to step back from the daily grind and ask the important, big-picture questions.

Who are our best customers? What are their common characteristics? What do their businesses "look, smell, and feel" like? Where are they located? Are they a particular size (e.g., in terms of revenue) or in certain vertical markets or niches where we have a higher rate of success? Where can we find potential customers with similar profiles?

Does our best chance for new business lie within our current portfolio of existing customers? How should we rank those current accounts and then segment our focus across various types of customers, based on growth potential? How much of our time should be allocated to account penetration, to prospecting, to working referral sources? Are there certain competitor's accounts that make sense to attack?

These are all highly significant and strategic questions, and I advocate the involvement of senior leadership in the decisions. The salesperson is entitled to input from management to ensure there's strategic alignment between the business and the sales effort, and management should certainly have a keen interest in how the sales organization is investing its time.

Time is the great equalizer and our most precious asset. Everyone needs to be on the same page regarding how time is being invested— particularly in terms of which accounts are being targeted to develop new business. Even the best talent will fail if too much time is wasted attacking the wrong targets.

Your Target List Must Be Finite, Focused, Written, and Workable

Beyond having a list of strategic targets to ensure we are calling on the right accounts, these other key parameters help maximize productivity and new business effectiveness.

A Finite List

A finite target list is essential for a successful new sales attack. Salespeople who succeed in acquiring new business lock in on a finite number of strategic targets. They're confident these prospects have been chosen for the right reasons, and they methodically work and rework that finite set of accounts. Over time, these successful hunters get noticed, get in, build relationships, and begin gaining traction. This only happens because they have committed to this defined list and are therefore able to penetrate targets with their sales weapons.

Too often I sit down with salespeople to review their target account list and am presented a pile of folders, trade publications, a local business journal *Book of Lists,* and printouts from various databases or industry directories. When I ask to see the *actual list* being used to pursue targets, they simple point to the pile and say, "This is my list." Oh boy.

Many salespeople fail because they're too quick to change direction. Frustrated about not getting a "kill" with the first shot, they forget about all the thought and prep work invested to create their original list. In frustration, they discard their lists and begin shooting in a completely different direction at a new set of targets. Typically, this redirection produces similar disappointing results, so they begin the cycle all over again, dooming their business development effort to failure.

A Focused List

In my own sales career and in others I've studied, periods of greatest success seem to result from a laser-focused sales effort. Focusing in on a vertical market or certain type of account yields many benefits. Repeated calling on the same type of company allows us to become "experts" as we learn the language, nuances, and business issues facing similar prospects. We become more comfortable and more confident. We know which questions to ask and when. We build a reputation along with an arsenal of case studies to demonstrate our credibility and worth. And it becomes easier and easier to replicate early successes.

During my time at the direct marketing company, I had a few quick victories selling our services to large advertising agencies. It didn't take long to figure out that these agencies were typically staffed with generalists in the production departments who were not experienced with the intricacies involved with producing a direct mail campaign. This lack of internal expertise would often get the agency in trouble, and I discovered how much value my team of experts could bring to these generalist production managers. It became readily apparent that these big agencies had a business problem for which my company had a perfect solution! After quickly picking up several new agency clients and seeing how pleased they were, I made an easy strategic decision to focus all of my time and energy pursuing agencies. That decision, along with the support the company provided, produced the record-breaking sales run I described in Chapter 1.

There's no prize for sales creativity or being known for selling into the widest variety of customer types. Find the path of least resistance and then focus like mad on that very path.

A Written List

It may sound crazy in the age of iPads, smartphones, and comprehensive CRM systems to ask salespeople to carry around or post a *written* target account list. Crazy, but effective. The most prolific new business developers live by their target lists. Whether handwritten and color-coded on an office whiteboard or neatly printed on an exported spreadsheet, top performers can point to their *finite, focused, written* list at any moment.

Scrolling through screen after screen of the CRM or thumbing through pages of an industry directory is not the same thing as pulling out a concise one-page list. I truly believe the very act of writing or printing out and posting a target list creates increased new business activity and improved results.

A Workable List

I'm regularly asked for an opinion on the right number of accounts for a salesperson to work. There are as many "right" answers to that question as there are types of businesses. It completely depends on the type of sale, sales role, and sales cycle. On one extreme, I have friends who sell enterprise-level IT solutions and are charged with selling to only a dozen or so accounts. At the far other end of the spectrum, I have worked with inside sales teams where each rep handled upwards of 400 accounts without skipping a beat.

Workable is the word I like to use. Target lists should be finite, focused, written, *and* workable. Too many accounts and they don't get the deserved attention. Too few and the salesperson runs out of targets to call and ends up surfing the Internet. Depending on the sales cycle, the level of difficulty gaining access to a prospect, and other account management responsibilities charged to the salesperson, the appropriate number of targets should be determined for a defined period of time. The key is to create a target list that can be worked effectively and thoroughly over that defined period.

Segmenting Your Existing Accounts

Although there are plenty of account-management-only-type sales roles, where reps are charged with growing business exclusively from their current customers, most of us in sales roles have the dual responsibility of managing (and hopefully growing) existing customer relationships and acquiring new business from new accounts. In either case, we must keep this truth in mind: *All accounts are not created equal.*

Too many outside salespeople operate in autopilot mode. They become complacent and don't invest the energy to dissect and segment their account list. Instead, they repeat the same route or rotation, working their accounts based on habit and convenience rather than opportunity. Some refer to this sloppy approach as doing "the milk run." Call it what you want. I call it lazy, foolish, and non-strategic.

I see a similar malady hurting the performance of inside reps. Rather than stepping back to see a big-picture view of their accounts, most activity and focus is determined solely by what comes up on the CRM's daily task list. In several companies, I've observed rep after rep focused exclusively on completing that day's call and e-mail list generated by the system. Don't get me wrong. In and of itself, completing your scheduled daily tasks is a good thing. But most reps do it in a robotic fashion with little perspective about the relative importance, or unimportance, of the specific accounts they're calling. In my opinion, inside reps would be better motivated and connected to the overall business if there was more macro thought put into how to focus attention to achieve greater results.

There's no law dictating how much energy and time we should commit to each customer. But since most of us in sales are judged according to the revenue growth we achieve, doesn't it make sense to allocate our attention to accounts with the greatest potential to produce results?

I advocate a very simple methodology for segmenting our customer lists. Assuming the salesperson knows his accounts (or territory, portfolio of clients, book of business, etc.), I suggest dividing the existing customers into four categories:

1. *Largest*—in terms of dollars spent (not size of the organization)

2. *Most Growable*—best opportunity for incremental revenue

3. *Most At-Risk*—highest probability of losing their business (some or all of it)

4. *Other*—accounts that do not qualify for any of the previous three categories

Some accounts will appear in more than one category. It's not uncommon to have a major account that's also one of your most at-risk customers either because of a competitive threat or something going on inside the account. And sometimes we find that our largest accounts have the most growth potential. Whatever the case, make those lists. Similar to my thoughts about having a workable number of targets, there's no right number of accounts to list in each category.

This exercise forces us to be more strategic and provides the salesperson an opportunity to make intentional decisions about the business instead of flying aimlessly on autopilot. If I'm getting paid based on sales results, you can bet I'm going to overserve and overinvest in my Most Growable, Largest, and Most At-Risk accounts. Along the same line of thinking, if a customer falls into the Other category, that account will not garner much time or mind share. Why should it?

I once worked with a brilliant consultant who talked a lot about *intentional imbalance*. What a great phrase that aptly communicates the point I'm emphasizing here. There are no prizes for salespeople who work really hard. The rewards accrue to those who move the dial, so it makes infinitely more sense to intentionally imbalance our focus toward the accounts where that's possible.

Preparing for Target Selection: The Who and Why Questions

In some sales positions, the list of target prospects is supplied to the salesperson. However, in the majority of small and midsize companies, that's not the case. Often, the challenging task of identifying and choosing potential clients is left to the salesperson. And that can be pretty daunting, particularly for a new hire.

I like to use a series of "who" and "why" questions to help identify strategic targets when creating a list:

- Who are our best customers (by industry, size, business model, location, etc.)?

- Why did they initially become customers? Why do they still buy from us?

- Who do we compete against in the marketplace?

- Why and when do they beat us? And why do prospects choose us over them?

- Who used to be our customers (said differently, who used to buy from us)?

- Why did we lose the business?

- Who almost became a customer but didn't (deals where we came close but lost)?

- Who has referred business to us in the past?

- Who should be referring business to us?

As discussed previously, selecting target prospects is one of our few chances to be strategic. We need answers to these questions in order to create a confidence-inspiring list of smartly chosen prospects and referral sources. I'd go as far as saying that building a great list is easy once we have these answers and just about impossible without them.

First and foremost, I want to pursue prospects that look, feel, and smell like our very best clients. We know we bring value to the equation. We have instant credibility. Our story is relevant and we have happy clients to prove it. If a salesperson isn't confident pursuing prospects that fit this profile, then he probably shouldn't be in sales.

To the seasoned new business developer, these best customer look-alikes are a softball down the middle. We should have no trouble getting in, asking the right questions, identifying opportunities, and telling a compelling story supported with case studies.

Making the Most of Referral and Indirect Selling

In certain sales roles, referral sources and decision influencers are more important targets than the actual end-user or purchaser. I've worked with an assortment of businesses where the greatest sales lift was achieved by a focused effort against a defined set of strategic referral sources. In this case, I'm not talking about the traditional method of seeking referrals from happy clients and people in our professional network. Rather, the actual targets are the collective group of potential referral sources.

Successful proactive loan officers continually work real estate agents to send clients their way for mortgages. Sales reps for general construction companies build intentional relationships with construction management firms that can recommend contractors to building owners. Premier bankers target personal bankers and tellers at local branches within their own banking organization, hoping they'll refer high net worth customers to them. Flooring sales reps call on architecture firms looking to get product specified for new projects, even though the actual "sale" is transacted with the flooring contractor. In all of these cases, it's imperative that the salesperson builds a *strategic, finite, focused, written,* and *workable* list of target referral sources.

If your personal sales success depends on indirect selling to key influencers and referral sources, it follows that you would have a specific plan of attack for this group of targets. The best reps treat this list as if their referral sources are the actual prospects. Accordingly, they monitor sales activity and results from the effort put against these influencers. One business development person at a client goes as far as segmenting his referral sources into four distinct categories.

He's committed to balancing his proactive sales attack across each category, and he tracks the number of meaningful conversations and referrals by type of referral source. Over time, his plan is to intentionally imbalance sales activity by favoring the types of sources that end up referring the best opportunities. That is a smart, strategic plan. No autopilot or milk run for that guy.

Resources for Identifying Targets

Once the strategic prep work is completed, it's time to identify the actual targets we'll pursue. Again, sometimes our own company is a great resource in helping to "name the names" for our lists. But often in smaller organizations, this responsibility falls to the individual salesperson. If you're new to business development and find yourself in that situation, fear not. There are plenty of highly valuable resources available to the business-to-business salesperson.

One of my personal longtime favorite resources is the local business journal. American Cities Business Journals (ACBJ), based in Charlotte, North Carolina, publishes a weekly business paper in more than forty markets across the United States. Each year, every local business journal compiles a *Book of Lists* for its market area. As a fan of identifying and sorting target prospects by company size and geography, the annual *Book of Lists* is a tremendously helpful tool. Want to see the twenty-five largest architectural firms or advertising agencies in a particular market? Want to scan the list of the fastest-growing privately held companies? No problem. You can purchase the entire *Book of Lists* (in printed or electronic format) or request only specific lists from desired markets. Looking for the largest employers or top 25 banks in Raleigh-Durham, Charlotte, and Atlanta? Place a single order with an ACBJ rep and have a spreadsheet with your requested data e-mailed to you within hours.

Hoover's, a Dun & Bradstreet company, is probably the best-known and most widely used online research platform for corporate data. Sales reps or sales teams subscribe to Hoover's and pay a yearly fee to research targets or compile customized lists based on user-defined criteria. While no online database is consistently 100 percent accurate, anecdotal evidence suggests Hoover's maintains the most up-to-date information on companies. It has outstanding customer support and regularly offers free trials that provide a peek into the power of a subscription. There are some new players competing in the same space and offering expanded feature sets, but after playing with a few, I'm sticking with my endorsement of Hoover's. Its ties to Dun & Bradstreet's perpetually updated database puts Hoover's in a unique position to provide highly accurate information.

LinkedIn is a must-have resource for every salesperson. It's the best liked, fastest-growing, yet still most underutilized tool for sales professionals. I can't possibly do justice to the power and versatility of LinkedIn in a brief mention here. I've read a few e-books and dozens of blog posts on the topic and my simple and strong admonition is that you do the same. It's easy to get started, connect with others, and begin exploring the myriad of ways to conduct research, build community, and initiate relationships. Most analogies fall considerably short when trying to describe the breadth and usefulness of LinkedIn. Update your profile and jump in.

Perhaps trade shows and industry associations are considered old-school methods for identifying target accounts, but I want to be where the prospects are. If virtually all the major players in an industry I'm targeting are exhibiting at a trade show, then I'll register as an attendee. It's typically costly to exhibit at a trade show, but relatively inexpensive to attend. Even if your specific contacts aren't physically present at the show, walking the aisles and meeting people at the booths of potential target accounts can be both an efficient and effective way to identify true prospects. Attending a trade show also provides you with opportunities to sit in a breakout session or keynote address, where you can gain a greater understanding of the hot issues faced by your target accounts.

Finally, don't ignore dinosaur-model industry associations. Some of the most active folks in these associations are wise old owls who

NEW SALES. SIMPLIFIED.

not only can impart wisdom, but also can connect you to major players in the industry. Modern sales philosophers will pooh-pooh the idea and suggest that you do most of your networking online. I couldn't disagree more, and suggest that the value of the association member directory alone is worth more than the annual price of admission.

Pursuing Your Dream Targets

When creating our target lists, I like salespeople to reserve a few spots for gigantic prospects. I first heard the term "dream clients" used by Chet Holmes, author of *The Ultimate Sales Machine,* during a keynote speech a few years ago. My friend Anthony Iannarino (who graciously provided the foreword for this book) regularly writes about the pursuit of dream clients on his award-winning site, TheSalesBlog.com. Dream clients are those monster accounts that, if landed, make your entire year and have the potential of changing the future of your company.

There's nothing quite like the celebration that ensues after closing a career-defining deal with a dream target. The first step in the process, sometimes years before the big celebration, is being bold enough to name the names and actually write down the handful of monster accounts that you'll commit to pursue. I've had the joy of closing a couple of these accounts myself, and I've also partied with client salespeople who reeled in the big one they declared a year earlier in a business plan.

There are two pieces of advice I want to share regarding dream clients. The first is to limit the selection. Pick just a handful, perhaps four or five, that you'll add to your target list. Once they're named, sketch out a unique mini-attack plan just for those targets. The key is to set aside a small percentage of time every week or two to advance the ball downfield with each dream target account.

The second piece of advice is cautionary. Because the pursuit of dream clients is a high-risk affair with low probability of success, it's essential that we continue to fervently work the normal targets on our list. The danger is falling in love with the notion of landing a dream client and ending up a *prisoner of hope* instead of working our sales process across the full list of targets. Winning a major deal with a dream client is as good as it gets, but we still need to make our numbers, even if that dream deal does not materialize.

Targeting Contacts Higher in the Customer Organization

Finally, I'd like to challenge you to think not only about which businesses you are targeting, but whom you should be targeting within those organizations. I encourage salespeople to pursue contacts higher up in the companies they target. Plenty has been written on this subject and for a good reason: It works! I've experienced success with this strategy in my personal selling efforts and also witnessed others significantly increase their batting averages by aiming for higher-level contacts at potential customers.

Less experienced, less successful, and less confident reps immediately feel increased anxiety when asked to consider targeting a contact who's positioned one, two, or even three levels higher up in the organization than they are accustomed to dealing with. It's easy to understand why the sales rep would be uneasy. It seems scarier going after higher-level management or senior executives. Some reps nervously proclaim they're having a hard enough time getting in to see their "normal" contacts, so how in the world could they have success going after the big guys?

Here's the counterintuitive dirty little secret: It's not harder and more frightening targeting higher-level contacts. It's actually easier and usually a lot more fun. The fear about moving up the ladder is artificially self-induced because of incorrect assumptions. It isn't like you know stories of sales reps who were once very successful prospecting with admins and purchasing agents but had their heads chopped off when they attempted to sell to the executive floor. I haven't seen reports about traumatized salespeople who were once quota-beaters but are now in therapy because of horrific experiences and the abuse dished out by gatekeepers and belligerent senior vice presidents. Have you? No, you haven't, because those stories are figments of our imagination. Salespeople scare themselves into believing they can't handle selling to higher levels in their target accounts, but there's no evidence validating those feelings.

You know what you typically find in the executive suite? Nicer people. Smarter people. More professional people. Bigger-thinking people. People more interested in achieving their goals than beating up a vendor over a nickel. Yup. In general, people who end up in executive positions got there because they were good. Most executives are a lot more concerned with solving business issues and achieving better results than they are with protecting their jobs or the status quo. That is a refreshing change, indeed!

The key to gaining the interest of senior executives is to be able to connect with them about issues that are on their mind. We must speak in the language they understand. Executives tend not to get involved in piddly crap and minutiae. They're certainly not interested in the details of your products or services. However, they are very interested in solving business problems and improving results in the areas under their control. To get an executive's attention, that is what we must be talking about, and it's why having a sharp, customer-focused sales story is essential.

If you're hesitant about attempting to shoot at significantly higher level contacts, answer this: What could happen if you tried it? Seriously consider the possible outcomes. What's the worst case? They ignore you or flat out tell you no. And how is that any different from the current status of that account? It isn't. You didn't have their business before you shot higher and now you still don't. Fine. You can still move forward and take your shot at the level you customarily target. They have no clue you missed the mark in the corner office. However, the reverse is not true. If you start at the lower level and get told no, it's infinitely harder to then take your pursuit up the ladder. That's how salespeople make enemies within the prospect organization. We can always scale our way back down the ladder, but it's very dangerous going over the head of people who believe they had the right and authority to tell us no.

The best thing that can happen is that you gain the interest of the higher-level contact and earn an opportunity to move forward. The next best scenario isn't so bad, either. In fact, I'd call it a minor victory. That's when the executive resonates with your approach and your story, but instead of inviting you to the table, she directs you to the appropriate person within her organization. In other words, she liked what she was hearing, but chose to send you to someone else better suited to evaluate what you're offering. Personally, I love when that happens. How much easier is that call or e-mail to the person the executive referred you to? "Hi, Kelly. It's Mike Weinberg. We haven't spoken before, but I was visiting with Susan Montgomery [the senior executive], and she asked me to connect with you about QRS." Or if that's a little bold for your comfort, tone it down by saying, "Susan suggested I reach out to you and thought you might get value hearing about how we help with TUV." Any approach that capitalizes on the internal referral is great and certainly places us in a stronger position than if we were initiating contact without it.

As a guy in my late twenties selling plastic components to manufacturers, I quickly learned it was a whole lot more fun and productive meeting with business owners and high-level management than it was to get beaten up by purchasing agents. Throughout my sales career that lesson has served me well. I challenge you to consider what type of preparation you would need to feel equipped to call on contacts higher up in your target accounts. I promise you it is worth the effort.

Questions for Reflection

► How closely does the profile of your "best accounts" align with the profile of the target accounts on your prospect list?

► What must be done to ensure your target list is *finite, focused, written,* and *workable*?

► If managing an existing book of business or territory, how can you better segment the accounts to ensure a focus on customers who can most greatly impact results?

► Which resources can you more effectively utilize to identify strategic target accounts?

► What would it take for you to get excited about targeting contacts higher up in your accounts?

Selecting targets is a critical first step in creating a new business development sales attack. Once we have our target list nailed, it's time to develop sales weapons to launch at these targets.

CHAPTER 6

Our Sales Weapons: What's in the Arsenal?

The expression "never bring a water pistol to a gunfight" reminds me of what the car dealer told me while delivering my first little Audi. After a comprehensive twenty-minute orientation covering the details of my finely tuned German machine, I asked if there was anything else I should know about driving the car. Excited to glean that last bit of wisdom from my personal Audi guru, and hoping to learn something I could brag about with my buddies, I listened with rapt attention as the salesman just smiled and said, "Don't race a Corvette; you'll lose."

While it wasn't the send-off message I was hoping for, it was a great piece of advice. Weapons matter. The better our weaponry, the more confidently we head into battle. My oldest son is a pro at the *Call of Duty: Modern Warfare* video game series. His mother doesn't like that he is in the basement shooting bad guys on the big screen. My take is a little different. I love when he shoots the bad guys; it's when he gets shot that I cringe. It is interesting to hear him talk about his favorite weapons and how he has become more proficient over time. My son's current weapon of choice is the Intervention sniper rifle. His sniping has significantly improved with practice and, because of his mastery of the Intervention, my son is confident of his chances of winning every battle.

The same truths apply to a new business development sales attack. Every salesperson must be armed with the necessary weapons and then become proficient at firing those weapons at target accounts. That is how we win the sales battle.

Salespeople not properly equipped for battle are less likely to engage with prospects. And those who are armed but ineffective at launching these weapons will either miss their targets completely or not get noticed when they do pull the trigger. You probably know several ill-equipped sales reps who are reluctant to engage prospects because they don't know what to do. And then there are the ineffective reps who are willing to pull the trigger but consistently take terrible shot after terrible shot; their feeble attempts fail to score a direct hit or move the sales process forward. Reluctant and ineffective are not words we want describing our sales effort.

Marshaling the Weapons in Your Arsenal

Visualize the salesperson as an elite fighter pilot. The mission: Acquire enough new pieces of business or new accounts to exceed sales goal. Once our pilot is locked into a strategic, finite, focused, workable list of targets (see Chapter 5), it's time to load the fighter jet with weapons required to execute the attack and carry out the mission. Here's a sampling of the weapons cache available for the sales battle:

➤ *Our Sales Story.* The story is foundational to everything we do in sales, and we use bits and pieces of it in all of our weapons. By "story" I'm referring to the language or talking points we use when asked what we do or when we tell someone about our business. It's so critical to our success that the next two chapters are dedicated to helping you create and implement a succinct, powerful, differentiating, customer-focused story.

▶ *Networking.* This is the age-old practice of building relationships and connecting with people who can help us. Networking is an art form for many veteran sales reps, whose packed Rolodexes are the equivalent to having a proverbial key to the city (for readers born after 1980, just substitute "electronic address book" for Rolodex).

▶ *Social Media.* The opportunity to research and connect with potential customers has exponentially increased with the social media revolution. While certain aspects of the Internet have made selling more challenging, tools like LinkedIn and Twitter are versatile weapons, providing information and opportunity to engage with prospects in ways that were unimaginable just a few years ago.

▶ *E-Mail.* E-mail has become the primary weapon of choice for many sales hunters when making an initial contact with prospects. It is less disruptive to the potential customer, and less reliant on the salesperson's ability to execute a proactive telephone call. Because it is less intimidating overall, e-mail can be a creative and effective entrée to an account.

▶ *The Proactive Telephone Call.* Much to the dismay of many Sales 2.0 pontificators and scared sales reps, I remain a huge fan of our old friend, the telephone. Bar none, the phone is still the most deadly and accurate weapon to score a face-to-face meeting with a target prospect. I attribute much of my own success as a new business salesperson to the quantity and quality of proactive phone calls (some ice-cold) made over the years. The concepts shared in Chapter 9 will provide everything necessary to help make you great on the phone.

▶ *Voice Mail.* Voice mail is reality, and anyone in sales needs to deal with it. I'm tired of all the whining about reaching a prospect's voice mail. If we're going to get voice mail more than half of the time, let's change our attitude about it. What a wonderful opportunity to drop a tidbit of our sales story, position ourselves as a value creator, and begin building a relationship. Yes, you can build a relationship with someone through voice mail messages.

▶ *Traditional Printed Marketing Materials.* Sell sheets, brochures, catalogs, and introductory letters to prospects sent via snail mail. These weapons have been around for ages and, when used properly, are still beneficial today.

▶ *Digital Marketing Tools: Blogs, Podcasts, Online Videos (YouTube), and Webinars.* These powerful and interactive tools put a modern twist on traditional sales materials. This relatively new genre of weapons is attractive for a variety of reasons, not the least of which is the incredibly low cost of production combined with the ease of updating content. Today's effective salesperson creatively deploys these tools to deliver ideas and value as appetizers that entice prospects to want to know more.

▶ *White Papers and Industry Experts.* Third-party, unbiased, or academic information can be launched before, during, and after the initial sales call to help pique a prospect's interest. Often, buyers are more receptive to information highlighting industry issues and marketplace realities from outside sources and respected gurus. It follows that a potential customer receiving this third-party information assumes that the salesperson providing the material has a meaningful solution to the issues presented.

▶ *The Initial Face-to-Face Sales Call.* The first face-to-face meeting with a prospect is the pinnacle of what we do in sales. The simple goal of all weapons launched beforehand is to set up the sales call. That's not true for the inside sales rep who conducts full sales calls over the phone. But for the outside rep, that initial meeting is the big enchilada—it's what we work so hard to achieve. Chapter 10 will help us prepare for the call, and Chapter 11 provides a fail-safe structure for conducting winning sales calls.

▶ *Probing Questions.* I'm convinced that more and better selling is accomplished by asking great questions than by making great presentations. Professional reps can significantly move the sales ball forward when they become proficient at asking pain-seeking, opportunity-uncovering, probing questions. And salespeople who are incompetent at asking questions will embarrass themselves and lose ground faster than one can imagine.

► *Case Studies.* The proof is in the pudding. I don't know where that expression originated, but it sure applies here. Case studies of how we've helped other clients are powerful evidence that what we sell is real and works. It's a thing of beauty when a salesperson weaves relevant case studies and client successes into the dialogue with a prospect.

► *Samples and Demos.* Sometimes a picture is worth a thousand words. Most salespeople are armed with samples and demos because these weapons are important to the marketing folks. While these materials are very effective when used well, I've seen too many examples of boring, self-focused demos blowing up in the salespersons hands.

► *Trade Shows.* While a costly and seemingly outdated platform, trade shows remain a viable and efficient way to connect live with large numbers of customers and prospects. All it takes is one meaningful lead becoming a major account and you become a fan of trade shows for life.

► *Facility Tours.* For many companies, their place of business is a memorable and differentiating sales weapon. The salesperson can provide the prospect with a great feel for his company's people, culture, and processes. One of my best friends and sales mentors sold 401(k) plans for a giant financial company. He had a reputation for turning the prospect site tour into a well-orchestrated selling science. Every step of the tour was planned, and he insisted that key players rehearse their roles.

► *Team Selling.* Top-performing hunters must become masters at using all available resources to win business. Team selling can take various forms. Personally, I love to drag the CEO or other senior executives along for high-level sales calls. The very presence of senior executives demonstrates commitment to earning the prospect's business and also helps keep the conversation focused on the buyer's business issues as opposed to the finer details of the deal. Another bonus of involving senior managers is that they become personally invested in the opportunity and usually make every effort to help you close the deal. It's also advantageous to use other subject matter experts (SMEs) from your company. In certain businesses, sales engineers, program coordinators, implementation specialists, or even account managers play essential roles in the sales process. This is particularly true in technical sales, where the sales rep is often seen only as the "relationship" person and the buyer prefers talking to technical experts.

► *Entertainment.* This is a main reason that a good number of people outside of sales resent those of us in sales. They hear about expensive dinners or seeming perks such as taking customers to ball games and they're jealous. Of course, they're not jealous of our having to call strangers on the phone, or getting stood up for meetings, or being stranded in airports because of flight cancellations. The truth remains that a ton of business is conducted away from the office and entertainment is a wonderfully effective weapon when used appropriately.

► *Presentations.* While I've come to hate the word *presentation* for good reason (see Chapter 13), presentations are expected or obligatory pieces of the selling process in many situations. When planned and executed properly, a killer presentation can be the difference maker that truly sets you apart from the competition. To be successful, we must perfect the art of drafting and delivering effective presentations.

► *Proposals.* Proposals come in all shapes and sizes. Sometimes we're forced to respond to a formal request for proposal (RFP), but in most cases we have the freedom to craft a highly customized document for our potential customer. Since the proposal is one of the final weapons we would fire at a target account, and since it's the one they can say "yes" to, it is certainly worth the effort to hone our proposal-writing skills.

► *References.* Right along with case studies, references serve as validation that we're as good as we say we are. Testimonials and third-party endorsements are more credible than anything we can say about ourselves, which makes cultivating usable references a worthwhile endeavor. It's ideal to have a variety of references so that you're in the advantageous position of being able to pick and choose the most relevant references for specific new business opportunities. And it's also perfectly acceptable to coach your references (assuming your relationship is solid enough) on what they should say or how they might be able to assist in winning over your prospect. The best sales reps maintain fantastic reference relationships and use them as deal-closing weapons whenever possible.

We have quite a stockpile of available weapons to launch a new business sales attack. Yet, of all the weapons I've listed, only a handful of them are truly "owned" by sales. Other weapons are developed and maintained by different parts of the organization and our role is simply to fire them, when appropriate, to help advance the sales effort.

In the next several chapters, we'll focus attention on the three mission-critical weapons that we fully control *and* which have the most dramatic impact on sales performance: the sales story, the proactive telephone call, and the face-to-face sales call.

Questions for Reflection

Scan through the list of weapons a few times and ask yourself:

- ► Which of these weapons are most applicable for your own new business sales initiative?

- ► What weapons are missing from your personal arsenal?

- ► Which weapons are loaded on your fighter jet but haven't been effectively deployed in battle because you're not yet comfortable using them?

- ► Which few weapons, if mastered, could most dramatically improve your effectiveness?

CHAPTER 7

Your Most Important Sales Weapon

Of all the sales weapons in our arsenal, none is more important than the sales story. When coaching, I spend more time working with individuals and sales teams to improve their story than on any other aspect of selling. The story is that critical.

We use the sales story in one way or another all day, every day. The story is foundational in the sense that it's incorporated into every other weapon. From marketing letters, e-mails, LinkedIn profiles, and telephone call outlines to voice mail scripts, initial sales calls, presentations, and proposals—all are built on pieces of the story. So, we must nail the story before we can arm ourselves with other weapons needed for battle.

A compelling, differentiating, client-focused story is a prerequisite for new business development sales success. It's our best opportunity to set ourselves apart from the competition; to beautifully package our offering; to gain the prospect's attention; and to position ourselves as experts, value creators, and problem solvers.

Most Companies, Executives, and Salespeople Don't Have an Effective Story

One of the most disconcerting and surprising discoveries I've found as a sales coach is that the vast majority of my clients did not have a uniform, coherent story that could be expressed by employees throughout their organization. When I walk into a company I'll typically ask the president, a handful of key executives, and a random sample of salespeople, "What can you tell me about XYZ Specialty Solutions?" I usually receive such varied responses that it causes me to wonder if they actually all work for the same organization. What I hear is usually pretty disturbing. Not only is everyone singing from a different hymnal, but what they're singing sounds awful.

It doesn't take a rocket scientist to conclude that a lame, ineffective sales story contributes to a sales rep's lack of confidence and lack of success in acquiring new business. (I'll come back to the effect the story has on a salesperson's demeanor at the end of this chapter.)

Another prevalent indicator that companies do not have an effective story is an over-reliance on marketing tools and toys. We shouldn't need a four-color handout to tell a prospect about our company. And there's a serious problem if it takes a projector and a dozen Power-Point slides to get someone interested in talking with us further. It should take a minute, maybe two, to tell our story, pique a prospect's interest, and begin a sales dialogue.

Consistency, reality, and integrity are all factors vital for an effective story. I've been witness to several situations in which the company attempted to manufacture a story for consumption in the marketplace. While that may work for a short period in print or on a website, a story that doesn't align with reality is bound to crumble in the hands of the sales team.

Salespeople are on the front lines. They know full well what customers experience when dealing with their company. A bogus story unsupported by the brand experience creates an embarrassing, stressful, and demotivating situation for the salesperson. It's also a huge deterrent to prospecting for new business.

One of my most infuriating experiences revolved around a CEO and the sales story. I was serving as the vice president of sales for a marketing services company and endured firsthand the confusion and pain that occurs when the story does not work. We were struggling with major changes in marketplace dynamics. For the better part of a year, our leadership team had attempted to revise its strategy. We met. We debated. We were desperate for clear direction and a cohesive story. The CEO created his own version of our story and imposed it upon the rest of us. He insisted we use specific words and descriptors that did not match our company's history or abilities.

It was a depressing year, full of sales disappointments. I was charged with leading a team that was frustrated and defeated. We no longer believed in what we were doing, our story stunk, and we knew we were in trouble.

I was contemplating my own future when our executive team flew out for a semiannual conference where we were regulars. There were 500 people in attendance at this two-day event. A powerful speaker had just concluded his talk and our CEO stood to ask a question. He introduced himself and was beginning to give a brief description of our company. We all expected to hear him parrot the sales story he had forced upon us. But he didn't even come close to using the words he required us to use. We were incredulous. He knew our story didn't hold water and was embarrassed to use it himself. How revealing. I couldn't sleep that night, and the next day confided in a colleague that I was done with this company and needed to move on.

Your Sales Story is Not About You

Newsflash: Everything's not about you. We were supposed to learn this important lesson as kids, but listening to salespeople wax on and on about their companies, it doesn't appear we got the message.

Think about it. Do you enjoy hanging out with people who are always talking about themselves? Do you listen intently to their every word, or do you begin to tune them out? Do self-focused people energize your mind and engage your heart? More likely, they bore you.

The same is true in sales. By far, the most common sin when it comes to telling the sales story is self-focus. I hear story after story after story from salesperson after salesperson—all about their own company, their offerings, their people, their processes. Borrrring.

Read this slowly: Prospective customers are not interested in what you do; they are only interested in what you can do for them. Said another way, no one cares how smart you are or how great you think your company is. They want to know what's in it for them. No one argues this point. When I share these concepts with clients, everyone nods and agrees. But intellectual assent to the concept isn't enough. That conviction must get carried into the sales story we use. In the next chapter, we will dive deep into creating a client-centered story built upon the foundation of what we achieve for our customers.

To drive home the point, I'd like you to test yourself and others at your company. Ask this simple question: What can you tell me about (insert your company name here)? How do you and your colleagues answer that question off the cuff?

The typical answer goes something like this: "We do this, that, and the other thing. We are privately held and have been in business for twenty-nine years. Our people are our most valuable resource and we are the best in our industry. We have unique processes and superior quality. Our customer service is outstanding, too." Notice anything? It's all about the seller.

Buyers are tired. Tired of being on the receiving end of presentations aimed "at" them. Tired of having their time wasted by unprofessional salespeople who promise great value but instead come to meetings and execute what I call the "show up and throw up"—regurgitating a load of rehearsed, canned, seller-focused marketing garbage. How can we break through the noise and overcome a buyer's indifference or negative response? Be darn sure to have a razor-sharp sales story. Stop talking about yourself and your company and begin leading with the issues, pains, problems, opportunities, and results that are important to your prospect.

Let me share a painful example of what not to do. Not long ago I received a note from a salesperson who had worked at a former client of mine. He had just joined a new organization and was blasting out a form e-mail announcing his new position and introducing the company. The content of that e-mail was so disturbing that I saved it for future coaching purposes. Here's an excerpt:

> *With decades of fulfillment, customer service, distribution, and returns management experience, HiddenName Company offers a set of expertise unavailable from traditional e-business vendors. Our footprint of more than 25 solution centers in 14 countries creates an unmatched global operating infrastructure enabling configuration and fulfillment of products sold online from the most strategic location, for rapid delivery with minimal cost.... HiddenName's e-Business Suite of Solutions offers brand owners and retailers a comprehensive set of integrated solutions. Services include e-commerce web store development and hosting, as well as a full suite of sales and marketing, customer support, financial management, fulfillment, and post-sales services. HiddenName integrates the technology, process, and service aspects of e-business....*

Just below that excerpt was a comprehensive flowchart using microscopic print to describe the company's world-class process.

You can't make this stuff up. Blah, blah, blah, blah, blah. Here's what I took from this example: "We do this, that, and the other thing. We are so stinkin' incredible that we feel the freedom to write record-length, self-absorbed, run-on sentence after sentence. It's all about us."

I was so embarrassed for the guy who sent it that I replied to the e-mail and suggested his first order of business should be fixing his new employer's obscenely self-focused story. Uncertain about whether I'd lose a friend or gain a client, I couldn't let the opportunity pass.

Telling the Story is a Lost Art: Whatever Happened to Puffery?

Storytelling is an important life skill. Look at how much time our kids spend in school learning how to write and edit stories. Everyone loves an interesting story, and we are all drawn to people who are wonderful storytellers.

Growing up as the son of a big-time New York sales executive, I had the advantage of hearing my dad talk about sales and watching him prepare for national sales meetings. He was big on "the story" and spoke with great passion and affection about the product his company sold. I remember him quoting the great Charles Revson, founder of Revlon, who said: "We don't sell cosmetics, we sell hope." What a fabulous line fostering the philosophy that it's not about the product or the company, but what could be achieved for the customer. My dad continually reminded salespeople that their main job was to help the customer win. When you speak the account's language and frame the sales story around what is most meaningful to the client, you stand out from the competition. Customers see you differently because the words you choose demonstrate a commitment to their success. That conviction was ingrained in me at a young age and is partly why I spend so much time drilling sales teams about the importance of their story.

Today, however, what I find in most companies is a very different attitude. Telling the story seems to be a lost art. Salespeople lack passion. They're sloppy with words; many of them seem disinterested in how they package their company and offering. Remember the days when salespeople were commonly accused of exaggerating the benefits of what they sold? Merriam-Webster defines *puffery* as "exaggerated commendation especially for promotional purposes." Whatever happened to puffery? I'm not advocating dishonesty in any way. What I am saying, though, is that we have gone way too far the other way and it's time to swing the pendulum back.

After all, packaging matters. The sales story is the "gift wrap" on our offering. It's the curb appeal of the house, the plating of an exquisite meal at a fine restaurant. It's the verbal explanation of our brand, the value we create, the experience we deliver. We should be enhancing, not diminishing, the perceived value of what we sell.

Differentiation and Justifying Premium Pricing

Why do so many salespeople sound alike? Why are so many of them saying the same thing, almost as if they're trying to blend in rather than stand out from the crowd? Same words, same boring technology demos, same droning webinars and predictable boardroom presentations. Same. Same. Same.

Perhaps people think that sameness is safe. I propose that the opposite is true: Sameness will kill us. Saying what everyone else is saying won't entice a dream prospect to give us an hour on an already-packed calendar. And if we do get the meeting, it certainly is not a compliment when the prospect can predict what we're going to say before we even click to the next slide.

When creating our story, differentiation is key. Differentiation gets people to listen. It's what breaks through the cacophony of inbound messages prospects receive every day. Differentiation helps earn us the meeting, creates intrigue, and opens the door for expanded dialogue. Even more critical, differentiation is essential to justify our premium price.

I've had the privilege of working with companies in a myriad of businesses, including printers, heavy manufacturers, security service providers, home builders, and high-end consultants. They come from industries ranging from food supply to banking to insurance. The one attribute that most of my clients have in common? They price their offerings at a premium to the market. It makes sense that the majority of companies seeking help for their sales teams are priced higher than the competition. If they had the lowest price, sales skill really wouldn't matter, would it? Instead, these companies intentionally position themselves above the competition and charge more for it. And this is as true as anything you will read in this book: *A premium price requires a premium story.*

Most salespeople talk a good game about not selling on price, but their actions reveal quite the opposite. How many times have we heard the lament "We lost it on price" from a defeated salesperson? My friend Mark Hunter (aka The Sales Hunter), from the great state of Nebraska, has released a powerful new book aimed at helping salespeople demonstrate value and protect their pricing and profitability. I highly recommend you check out *High-Profit Selling: Win the Sale Without Compromising on Price.*

This must be absolutely clear: It's our job and responsibility to justify the delta between what our company charges and the price of alternatives available in the marketplace. That's what we're paid for. If it always comes down to price, our companies wouldn't need salespeople! "Come and get it. We've got the lowest price anywhere." doesn't require a value-adding (and costly) salesperson. There are sound reasons why our best customers happily pay more for our services. The burden of proof rests on us, and we must accept the fact that articulating value is our job.

A Great Story Produces Confidence and Pride

A powerful sales story can change the attitude and the outlook of an entire sales organization. I've seen it happen and it's a thing of beauty. A client president shared with me how their new story became a game-changer for his firm. It completely transformed the way the company's executives felt about approaching Fortune 500 prospects. Another client bragged about how well his company's rookie sales team handled conversations at a large trade show just weeks after being armed with a new and improved story. This client kept repeating, "I wish you could have heard them. They were so confident talking with buyers at the show."

When our story is right, it puts us in the proper mindset to prospect for new business. The entire dynamic of the sales process changes when we view ourselves as problem solvers and value creators who are armed with a story that helps us clearly communicate to potential customers. We enter into the sales conversation with great optimism because we believe the prospect should want to talk with us.

Consider your own level of confidence as you engage a prospect. If you're not as optimistic as you'd like, it is probably because you doubt the effectiveness of your story.

When salespeople love their sales story, it creates in them a great sense of pride. My former consulting partner Donnie was a master at understanding the heart of a salesperson. He would constantly preach that sales performance is as much a matter of the heart as it is of the mind. Sales is not accounting. We cannot just work the process and trudge through the day even when we're down or don't believe in what we are doing. Our job requires connecting with people; building trust; capturing attention; and demonstrating passion, enthusiasm, and pride. What a difference it makes when our hearts are fully engaged, because we're as proud as can be of the company we represent. Nothing can create that sentiment better than an effective, powerful sales story.

Now let's take a look at how to craft this compelling, differentiating, client-focused story we desperately need.

Questions for Reflection

> ► If you sat down with a few key executives and salespeople from your company and asked each of them to share your company's story, what would you hear?

► Take some time to read through letters, e-mails, and even proposals you have provided to customers and prospects recently. Is the content more about your customers and what you can achieve for them, or is it more focused on your own company?

► How satisfied are you with the sales story you currently use? What is missing, and how could the story be more effective?

CHAPTER 8

Sharpening Your Sales Story

Think for a minute. What makes a story interesting or compelling?

Stories that pique our interest and garner our attention are those that draw us in. Wouldn't you agree the stories that are most captivating are the ones where you can imagine yourself as part of the story, or perhaps feel jealous that you are not?

The same applies when dealing with our sales story. I benefited from having mentors like my dad and my boss, Danny Abraham, the chairman and CEO of Slim-Fast. Both men were absolute masters at framing the story. The customer was always the main character and centerpiece of their sales pitch. But as I began to observe other salespeople, I noticed most were not very good when it came to telling their story. In fact, most of them had a hard time grasping and maintaining a buyer's attention. The biggest difference was that, unlike Danny or my dad, these salespeople were totally focused on their product and why it was so wonderful as opposed to issues important to the customer. When I transitioned into sales, I followed the lead of my mentors, whose effectiveness convinced me that selling was about the customer and their needs, desires, and issues. As my career progressed and I had more sales calls under my belt, I became more and more convinced that most customers couldn't care less about what we do. However, they were incredibly interested in what our products or service could do for them.

Our Story Must Pass the "So What?" Test

As important as this profound sales truth is when dealing with existing customers, it's magnified exponentially when trying to gain the attention of a prospect. So many people in sales lead with statements such as "We make" or "We are suppliers" or "We do this, that, and the other thing." And when salespeople lead in this manner, buyers are almost immediately thinking: "So what?"

I encourage you to try the "so what" test. Listen to another salesperson on the phone attempting to earn an appointment with a tough prospect. Or accompany a rep on sales call. Every time the salesperson makes a statement, simply ask yourself, "So what?" It's very convincing when we begin to realize how much of what we regularly say is self-focused drivel that has no real meaning to the customer.

What happens when we the start our pitch by talking about what we do? The prospect thinks or may even say aloud, "We already have that." We already have a banking relationship. We already have a widget supplier. We already have an advertising agency. We already have someone cleaning our data center. Fill in what your company does: We already have a _____. In all likelihood, your prospects think they have it covered.

Bestselling author Jill Konrath speaks about the challenge of getting the attention of today's crazy-busy prospects in her superb book *SNAP Selling*. I love the mental picture created by the phrase *crazy-busy prospects*. We are not earning a spot on a crazy-busy prospect's calendar by talking about our offerings (with a possible exception if there is an Apple logo on our product). Breaking into a prospect's world is only going to happen when we talk about something that matters to them.

Three Critical Building Blocks for a Compelling Story

There are three critical sections, or building blocks, to a compelling sales story:

1. Client issues addressed

2. Offerings

3. Differentiators

Customer/client issues, the first building block and bedrock of our compelling sales story, refers to:

► Customer pains we remove

► Client problems we solve

► Opportunities we help customers capture

► Results we achieve for clients

Offerings, our second building block, simply state *what* we sell (emphasis on simply). Our offerings are what we do—the services, solutions, or products for which we bill customers.

Differentiators, the third building block, explain *why* we are better and different from other alternatives. This final building block provides solid reasons why we are the best choice to address the client's issues, as listed in the first section of the story.

These three building blocks are all necessary to craft a succinct, compelling, client-focused sales story. And the sequence matters—a lot! As important as the actual components themselves is the order in which we use them.

Why Lead with Client Issues?

The issues we address for clients serve as the lead-in to our sales story because that's where the power is derived. Client issues are the sharp tip of our sales spear. No one cares what we do, how smart we are, or how special we think our company is. Sad, but true. It's not about us. Prospects are interested in one thing: What's in it for them. We lead with the pains we remove, the problems we solve, and the results we achieve for customers because those things are important to them. They're relevant. These issues draw people in. They shake prospects out of their slumber and help delay their reflex resistance to our sales pitch.

A whole lot of salespeople make the mistake of leading with their offerings. That's the worst thing we can do. It screams "commodity" to the buyer. It also communicates that the most important part of the conversation is about what we sell. "I'm the sales rep and I am here to tell you about we do." Awful. And way too common.

Some salespeople like to lead with differentiators, which I'll admit is better than charging into battle with your product front and center. But differentiators are still about us and why we're so great. If there are dramatic reasons our solution is better and different, it's possible we'll capture a prospect's attention. But there's still a good chance that our differentiators are not meaningful to the prospect. And there remains the risk that we'll be viewed as self-absorbed braggarts only concerned with expounding on why we're so great.

When we lead with client issues, we get a prospect's attention fast. We're talking about what's likely on the other person's mind. We also set ourselves up as problem solvers. By talking about the clients' needs first, we position ourselves as professionals who can address *their* issues.

Another benefit of leading with client issues is that it sets us up to ask probing questions about those very issues later in the sales process. In a sense, we foreshadow where we plan on taking the sales conversation. When the first things out of our mouth (or in writing) communicate to the prospect that we are all about addressing *their* issues, the dynamic of the sales dance radically changes. We're no longer viewed as the typical product-pitching sales rep that buyers try to avoid at all cost. Instead, we're seen as experts with solutions positioned to open a dialogue about the issues on the prospect's mind.

Leading our sales story with issues has one final practical application: It helps us qualify the prospect. If potential customers have no pain, no problems in need of solving, and are not trying to achieve a different result, then why would they make a change? If nothing is wrong or in need of improvement, why bother? Businesses and people don't change direction for no reason. If we take our best shot describing the reasons our customers turned to us and can't get a reaction or interest from the buyer, then the sales conversation is pretty much over. No Issues = No Sale. If the issues we address don't interest them, there's no reason to talk about what we do or why we're different. Just move on to the next prospect.

Drafting the Power Statement

I created what I call "The Power Statement" as my answer to the elevator pitch and the value proposition, two annoyingly overused expressions that mean different things to different people. Last time I checked, there was not a whole lot of business being transacted in elevators. So it doesn't make sense trying to cram our sales story into a format designed for use between the lobby and the ninth floor.

Something wonderful, powerful, and magical happens when combining the three building blocks of our story under a brief headline and a transitional phrase. I've used this formula with more than fifty companies and continually receive unanimous positive feedback on its transformative power. Once complete, the power statement serves as a one-page, two- to three-minute encapsulation of our sales story. It can be used by itself in full form when speaking with someone face-to-face (on sales calls) or when elements from the power statement are excerpted for use in other sales weapons (telephone, voice mail, e-mail, presentations, proposals, etc.).

Let's take a look at the construction of the power statement and then review two examples.

Headline

The headline is a one- to two-sentence introduction. It helps provide context and allows your audience to place you in a category to better digest your story.

Transitional Phrase

This brief phrase sets the stage to grab your contact's attention. It opens the door to share the client issues your business addresses. It starts with either the type of business you are pursuing or the position of the contact you are addressing. For example:

GHI companies turn to (Your Company Name Here) when....

Or:

Senior marketing executives look to us (or Your Company Name Here) when they....

This type of lead-in is a shrewd technique that allows us to speak in the third person about what we accomplish for our customers. Instead of simply declaring our results in a brash or braggadocio fashion, we make compelling points about why our customers look to us for help. In a sense, the transitional phrase couches our strongest selling points as if they were a testimonial coming from our best clients.

Client Issues / Pains Removed / Problems Solved / Results Achieved

This section of the power statement lists between three and seven client issues we address. Use a conversational, bulleted format, describing each issue briefly using provocative or emotionally charged words. For instance:

➤ Striving to achieve Result 1.

- ► Frustrated from dealing with Pain 2 and ready to take action.

- ► Under significant pressure to eliminate Problem 3.

- ► Committed to accomplishing Result 4.

- ► They've had it with Pain 5.

- ► Facing threats (or regulatory pressure) from Issue 6.

- ► They are finally tired of living with Problem 7 and want help tackling it.

Offerings

This very brief section of the power statement is where we rattle off what it is we actually sell. It works best to simply describe our offerings in a few sentences, being careful not to embellish or oversell here. Our offerings are the least compelling component of our story, and that is why this section is short and sandwiched between the client issues we address and our differentiators.

Differentiators

The power statement concludes with a strong list of reasons that we are the best choice to address the client issues we previously described. This is our opportunity to brag and declare why our offerings are better than other options available to the customer. I suggest leading into a list of at least five differentiators with an intriguing sentence. For example:

(Your Company Name) continues to grow (or dominate our space) because we are very different from what you will find in the marketplace...

Differentiator 1

Differentiator 2

Differentiator 3

Differentiator 4

Differentiator 5

A Couple of Sample Power Statements

The best way to help prepare you to create your own power statement is to share a couple of real-life examples. This first one is from a long-time client headquartered in Toronto, Ontario. The company, which I've fictitiously renamed Allsafe Security, provides a full gamut of security services to business clients across Canada. Allsafe maintains offices in Toronto, Calgary, and Vancouver, and the large sales team is comprised mostly of former security officers who moved up through the ranks. The company has a stellar reputation in the marketplace. Commensurately, its services are priced at a significant premium and Allsafe faces regular price-cutting attacks from competitors.

When my partner Donnie and I were brought in, the sales force was demoralized from several sales leadership transitions and failures. But the team was committed to succeeding, and it was obvious right away how much these guys loved Allsafe. Because the salespeople had come up through the ranks, they were experts in the business, and passionate about the services they offered. All this sales organization needed was love, direction, focus, and a much improved sales story to justify the premium pricing.

We facilitated a few sales meetings to begin reenergizing the team. I rode shotgun with a few of the better reps and sat in on a dozen or so sales calls to get a flavor of the business. We scanned a few winning and losing proposals and reviewed every available piece of sales literature. Then we tackled their bloated, grandiose, pompous, and self-absorbed sales story. After conducting a few exercises to garner everyone's best thoughts, here's the power statement we came up with.

Allsafe Security Power Statement

HEADLINE

Allsafe is the premier security services provider in Canada. We work with building owners, property managers, and individual corporations to deliver true integrated security.

TRANSITIONAL PHRASE AND CLIENT ISSUES ADDRESSED
Building owners look to Allsafe when:

► Seeking a competitive advantage by offering the finest security available to tenants and guests.

► Frustrated that their current system is not doing what was promised when it was "sold" to them.

► Facing excessive liability exposure and growing life/safety fears.

► Continually embarrassed by the image projected by their security personnel.

► They've had it with guards who are poorly trained, unreliable, and constantly turning over.

► They're searching for a truly integrated solution combining manpower, system monitoring, and CCTV.

► There is no peace of mind regarding a potential emergency; the current provider lacks the appropriate resources, coverage, and experience to handle a crisis.

Before continuing with the final two components of Allsafe's story, let's pause here to drive home a few points. What struck you when reading through this critical part of their story?

The two-sentence headline is simple, direct, and clear. Allsafe is not confused about what it does or the market it serves. Anyone unfamiliar with the company would quickly grasp the basics and have context to process the balance of the story. It seems like a no-brainer, but I'm continually amazed how challenging it is for many salespeople and executives to succinctly articulate exactly what it is their company does. And if we can't explain it clearly, then we should not expect a prospect to understand it, either.

It's been years since we crafted this power statement, and I still get excited reading that client issues section. Let me ask you to imagine yourself as the senior property manager for a major corporate campus. The buck stops at your desk for all matters related to the safety and protection of 3,000 employees who work for the corporate clients at your site. Would that list of issues Allsafe addresses grab your attention and draw you in? You bet it would, because those are the very things on your mind every day.

What else struck you about the client issues section of the power statement? Isn't it interesting that there's not one single thing about Allsafe? Not one word about what Allsafe does or how the great the company is. Every single syllable is focused on issues that matter deeply to the prospective customer. Never forget that the power in the power statement comes from listing the pains we remove, the problems we solve, and the results we help clients achieve. After sharing these issues, prospective customers are much more likely to listen to the balance of what we have to say and more willing to answer our probing questions. We've successfully set the stage, and possibly the hook. Let's continue with the final two pieces of Allsafe's power statement.

OFFERINGS

We provide true integrated security. Allsafe services include first-class manpower, access systems, monitoring, mobile response, and closed-circuit television.

DIFFERENTIATORS

Allsafe continues to dominate the security market because we are very different from the other available alternatives:

- ► We are a true one-stop shop that provides real integrated solutions.

- ► We offer in-house financing and leasing options help clients manage capital expenditures and cash flow.

- ► We are "vendor agnostic," allowing us to provide the best-fit products for your particular application.

- ► No one handles crisis situations better or responds faster. It is our specialty.

- ► We have, without question, the most professional, polished, responsible, and courteous officers in the business; clients tell us that our officers are like their own key employees.

- ► Our clients don't leave us. And the very few that did came back.

Of all the clients I have been blessed to consult, Allsafe was probably the most energizing and fun. The team took to coaching well and was primed to deliver impressive results. Everything felt right, and in our second year of the engagement, the CEO challenged us to give up some fee in consideration for a significant bonus based on net new business acquired. We believed in the sales talent and the company's ability to deliver, so we jumped at the chance to have skin in the game. It turned out to be a brilliant decision. We earned more stamps in our passport than we could count and a bonus that was more than double what we would have made from a straight fee. I credit a good portion of that team's sales success to the formidable story we created and each salesperson's willingness to incorporate it into the sales attack.

As a coach, I am happy to take my own medicine and practice what I preach. In order to provide another example, here is the power statement I am currently using for my own business. Now that you have the gist, I'll leave out the section titles.

The New Sales Coach Power Statement

I am a sales coach, consultant, and speaker. I specialize in new business development and turning around sales teams for midsize organizations.

Chief executives (or companies) bring me in when...

- ► They are looking to create a team of proficient sales hunters and take their new business development attack to new levels.

- ► The sales team is not working the way it is supposed to.

- ► Sales results are not what they should be, or the company is not acquiring new business at the desired rate.

- ► Sales leadership feels the team is stuck in a rut and in need of fresh ideas and outside perspective—particularly around proactively developing new business.

I provide sales and sales leadership coaching to sales teams and sales managers, sales force consulting to senior executives, and speak on a variety of topics pertinent to succeeding at new business development. I am typically hired by companies, but in the right circumstances work with individuals.

Clients experience tremendous success and rave about my work because my approach is very different from what you normally find...

1. I use an über-simple approach and new business development framework, and I speak in blunt, plain language.

2. Don't call me for customer service training because I won't do it, and there are better choices if you are looking to

---

improve the babysitting skills of account managers. You only want me if you are serious about increasing New Sales.

3. I roll up my sleeves and get dirty working with your team and learning your business; I will not bring your people to my classroom and subject them to some franchise's pre-prepared, canned training content. Don't be surprised to find me jumping in your sales reps' cars to observe sales calls and coach in the field.

4. As Alan Weiss shared at a conference last year, you don't want a ski coach who sits in the lodge sipping brandy and talking ski theory. You want someone who grabs you and says, "Follow me down the hill." I've been the No. 1 guy in three companies and will model every sales concept and behavior I coach.

5. I am a consultant by choice after walking away from a lucrative sales executive job. Helping salespeople and sales teams acquire new accounts is my passion, and I believe I can more effectively create sales lift from outside a company than as an employee.

6. You will get the truth about your people and your sales model. Once I discover someone is never going to succeed in sales, I won't allow you to pay me to coach them. I will also look CEOs in the eye and plainly tell them what they are doing that is hampering the sales effort. Often, coaching evolves into consulting when issues emerge that must be addressed.

7. It is personal. When you engage me, I behave like my livelihood depends on your sales success.

For what I sell, it has been effective to stick with fewer, broader client issues and provide a more detailed list of differentiators. I think that's due to the fact that almost every company experiences some of the pains and problems I outline. It's relatively easy to draw a prospect in by listing those issues. Everyone wants more sales, and most teams are not firing on all cylinders.

However, because there are so many trainers and sales improvement gurus out there, I find that most CEOs want to understand why I'm different and more effective at solving a sales organization's problems than all the others claiming to have the answers.

My power statement does exactly what I need it to. It gives me confidence to talk with anyone about what I do. It positions me as someone who understands the issues facing sales teams today. It's compelling enough to draw potential customers into a dialogue. It paves the way to ask opportunity-seeking questions. And it keeps me on message. My story is my story is my story.

The Sales Story Exercise

After you've read these two examples of compelling sales stories, my hope is that you're chomping at the bit to begin work on yours. It can be a messy process, but I promise that the result is well worth your time and energy.

You'll need some blank paper and access to whatever sales and marketing literature you have (e.g., brochures, sell sheets, catalogs, recent proposals, and copy from your website). Experience shows that it's helpful to go through this exercise with others. So if you're part of a sales team, see if you can get everyone together for an hour-long initial session. If you're not part of a team, try to gather a few key people from your company that have an interest in seeing you sell more. If you are a solo-practitioner like I am, it's fine to do this exercise on your own. There are some key questions you can ask current and past clients whose answers will provide great fodder for your story.

Start with three blank sheets of paper. We'll use them for a brain dump to create exhaustive lists for each of the three main sections of the power statement: one sheet each for client issues, offerings, and differentiators.

I like to tackle the client issues section first. It is the most critical and usually takes the most effort to get right. Most salespeople are accustomed to talking about their offerings and differentiators, so it often takes more practice to frame up the client issues list appropriately. As with any good brainstorming session, don't overthink it. Write down every thought that comes to mind. There's plenty of time to delete the dumb items and wordsmith the good ones later in the process. Even before scanning your sales and marketing literature or talking with clients, start by writing answers to these questions on your client issues sheet:

▶ Why did your best customers initially come to you?

▶ What business problems were they facing?

▶ What results were they looking to achieve?

Once you have a solid list started, move on to the next set of questions. These questions help you dig a little deeper into the client issues you address:

▶ What pains are your potential customers likely to experience by choosing or staying with the wrong provider (your competition)?

▶ What problems do you see prospects experiencing from trying to do for themselves what you should be handling for them (self-performing versus outsourcing)?

▶ Which opportunities might they miss or which results will fall short because they are not your customer? Said another way, what is the opportunity cost of not working with you?

Now that you, and possibly your teammates, have exhausted your creativity, it's time to get some outside help. Call your absolute favorite customers, the ones who are advocates and raving fans. Don't e-mail them but call them. You want to hear their voice inflection, emphasis, and emotion. Let them know you're working on sharpening your sales story and would be honored if they would help. Ask these customers:

► Why did you come to us in the first place? What were you looking to achieve?

► What issues were you looking to address?

► Why do we still have your business? (Listen carefully to these answers because you might get some bonus material to use on your differentiators list.)

► How have we made your life and business better?

You should be on cloud nine after speaking with a few customers. If this feedback doesn't increase your confidence, nothing will. What a double treat: Your customers are reminding themselves why they love you, and you get to incorporate their words into your sales story. It doesn't get any better than that.

Finally, scan through your marketing materials. Pull out great phrases that speak to the business issues your company addresses for customers. Be careful not to get lulled into listing reasons your company is so wonderful. Find the gems describing what you achieve for customers and incorporate those into the giant list you've been creating.

At this point you likely have a page chock full of reasons that customers turn to your company. If you're doing this exercise along with others, now is the time to have them share what they feel are their best items. I like to start a fresh Word document and project the compiled list onto a screen for the group to review, edit, delete, and combine bullets.

The sales group is usually amazed at how broad and strong are the reasons that customers look to/turn to/trust their company. Argue the list down to the seven or so best "client issue" bullets. Then you can start wordsmithing, nuancing each bullet into a format that nicely follows the transitional phrase: *"X type of companies or Y type of contacts turn to Your Company Name when looking to..."* or *"They look to us when facing...."* Make an effort to incorporate compelling, emotional, or provocative words or phrases to describe your client's experience. For instance, customers are exhausted from, frustrated with, challenged by, have had it with, are fearful of, pressured to, or are desperately trying to achieve some result. (Okay, "desperately" might be a little over the top, but you get the idea.)

Once you've refined the list to the point where it is ready to insert into the power statement, move on to the differentiators section. This section tends to come more naturally and go faster than the client issues page. List all the reasons that you believe your company, product, service, or solution is better and different. Cover the gamut of reasons, from culture issues through technical expertise, proprietary processes, and service guarantees. Don't forget to include yourself and the difference you bring to the table for clients. In some cases, the salesperson is one of the most significant differentiators in the equation. Toot your own horn if you're helping to set your offering apart. Review, edit, and sharpen what you came up with until you have a strong list that you love.

The offerings section should take less than five minutes to complete. If you can't rattle off exactly what it is you sell, what you send invoices for, then there's a bigger problem. Craft a couple of direct sentences and insert them between the client issues section and the differentiators.

Congratulations. You now have the first draft of your much-improved sales story. In most cases, it takes a few weeks of tweaking and revising to get it where you want it. Carry it around for a while and keep tinkering with it. In one case, my client and I continued to play with their new power statement for about a month. After the fifth revision we both agreed that we had it nailed.

What We Can Do Now

There's one important point about the power statement I've yet to mention. The power statement is an internal document, not a handout. It's for internal use only. The power statement becomes an invaluable source document for creating other sales weapons. It provides the talking points or copy highlights we need in various situations. In fact, once we have a power statement we love, it's amazing all we can do with it.

The power statement is a fantastic resource from which we're able to pull excerpts. Need to write an introductory letter to a prospect? Grab the power statement and trim off just a touch of the fat. Put a salutation at the top, follow the same progression (a headline followed by client issues addressed, then the offerings, wrapped up by differentiators), and close the letter by letting the prospect know you would love to visit with the company, to see if you might be a fit to help with some of these very issues. Sign your name at the bottom, and boom, you have the strongest sales letter you've ever sent.

If you want to send a brief series of e-mails as part of a drip campaign, the power statement is where you start. You can personalize a brief introduction and then pivot to a transitional phrase before dropping in just a couple of key issues you address for clients. One slight alteration to the transitional phrase that works well in a brief e-mail goes something like this:

We serve logistics managers (or another appropriate contact position) who are telling us they're facing Issue No. 1, which requires immediate attention, or they are working to solve Issue No. 2, which if not addressed is causing Issue No. 3.

I might choose to include an offering or two and possibly one differentiator, but I would stop there in an e-mail. You could follow up with a second e-mail a week later. This time repeat just one of the same client issues from the first e-mail and pick out a different issue from your power statement to go with it.

In the next chapter there's a section dedicated to creating a mini power statement to use when proactively telephoning prospects. Strong talking points are an effective confidence booster for sales reps who are scared to call prospects on the phone. Not only can we arm the salesperson with a superb mini power statement, but the balance of the full version is available as a resource if the phone call develops into a full-blown sales conversation.

A completed power statement also serves as a perfect guide to craft probing questions for the discovery part of our sales calls. Start with the bullet points you wrote describing the client issues you address, then turn them around by rephrasing the statements as questions. Using Allsafe Security as the example, here are some easily created open-ended, issue-seeking questions:

- ► What do you wish your current security system could do that it isn't doing now?

- ► Tell me about the last few significant safety events. Where was the security lapse, and what was the reaction of your tenants?

- ► We often hear about security guards embarrassing building management. What are some of the behaviors of your current guards that you would like to see changed or improved?

- ► Under your current setup, what happens when a true emergency strikes? Who will respond and how will it be handled?

The Commodity Antidote

My clients run the spectrum from high-end consulting and professional service firms to small manufacturers in businesses that are highly commoditized. I have a blast helping salespeople in commodity-type businesses use elements of their improved sales story to communicate value and differentiation to customers.

The power statement provides a way to articulate the meaningful reasons (other than price and availability) that customers buy from you. That's a big deal when a buyer's first two questions are "Do you have it in stock?" and "What's your best price?" The reality is that very few products and services are true commodities. Although the product or service may be perceived as highly price sensitive, salespeople certainly don't help themselves by jumping to the price conversation so quickly. But that doesn't mean that price is the only factor influencing the buying decision.

Your power statement gives you ammunition. One of my clients has started to capitalize on a few selling points that its reps previously were taking for granted. The company is a small distributor of perceived commodity items in a niche business. Its competitors are giant organizations. When you call the competition for help you get the dreaded automated attendant. After angrily punching keys trying to get to a human being, your call is directed to a sales pool. In other words, no one there knows you. You have no consistent point of contact and must struggle through an interactive voice response system every time you call. My client has a real person answer 100 percent of the calls during business hours, and every customer is assigned to a dedicated account team. As part of the outbound sales call, the inside reps make darn sure to make prospects aware that "a lot of our ABC type customers look to us because they've had it with automated voice mail; they want to talk with a real person; and they come to really appreciate that we assign them a dedicated account team who gets know them and their business." Following that client issue statement, they jump to a couple of differentiators: "We are ridiculously easy to work with, from instant account setup to low minimums. We're looking for long-term relationships, not just orders. Our commitment is that we'll never try to oversell you a more expensive piece of equipment or load you up with more supplies than you need."

Yes, my client sells virtually the same product as its competitors. And most people it sells to are keenly interested in talking about price. The reps have begun to change the focus of sales conversations from price to the reasons companies buy from them. Let me ask, after hearing just a few snippets of their sales story, would you be willing to at least consider paying a few pennies more to buy from them? I would!

Our sales story is our most important and most frequently used weapon. When we have a great story, it changes everything.

Questions for Reflection

➤ Before reading this chapter, how were you framing your sales story for prospects?

➤ What messaging have you been using to capture a prospect's attention, and how effective has that message been?

➤ Who inside your company would be valuable to include in the sales story exercise?

➤ Once you have your power statement nailed, how do envision yourself using it?

CHAPTER 9

Your Friend the Phone

The dreaded cold call. I won't even refer to it as a cold call anymore. The term causes such an immediate negative and visceral reaction in most salespeople that I made the executive decision to rename it "the proactive telephone call."

This is the most requested coaching topic in my practice. And it's probably safe to bet that a good number of you reading this book scanned the table of contents and turned directly to this chapter. For whatever reason, the phone creates all kinds of weird emotions and mental blocks for salespeople, yet everyone wants coaching on making better phone calls. Studies suggest that public speaking is one of the most feared activities, but I meet reps all the time who would choose to make a speech in front of a giant crowd over having to call a prospect on the phone.

Let me start by admitting right up front that I don't love making proactive telephone calls to new prospects. I do it, and I've done it for a long time. I'm very good at it. But it's far from my favorite sales activity. Nonetheless, it's a necessity for salespeople charged with developing new business. That's why I spend a ton of time helping clients with their proactive calls, and why I still do it myself.

In Chapter 1, I touched on the dangers of the false teaching coming out of the Sales 2.0 camp. But I don't want to throw the baby out with the bathwater. There are plenty of quality ideas and sales methodologies emanating from this movement. However, I feel obligated to warn that the worst myth being perpetrated by the 2.0 crowd is that we no longer need to make proactive telephone calls to prospects. What makes it so dangerous is that it's exactly what so many reluctant prospectors want to hear. It's a readily accepted false teaching because it provides a wonderful excuse not to do one of the most important yet incredibly unpopular sales tasks.

Trust me. If inbound marketing was a magic bullet and perfect panacea for creating demand, then we could stop proactively pursuing target accounts. But it isn't. Anyone who is intellectually honest and not employed by an inbound marketing company will admit: It's a fantasy that search engine optimization (SEO), Facebook, and tweeting about our community-building, value-creating blog are sufficient to produce the volume of face-to-face sales meetings required to hit our new business objectives. Fantasy, plain and simple. Inbound marketing is a magnificent supplement to, but not a replacement for, one of our most potent sales weapons—the outbound proactive telephone call.

Now that we're all in agreement that making proactive calls is an essential component of our new business attack, let's dig into what I like to call "the keys to calling." Since we need to make calls, it would be nice if we didn't freeze up, freak out, and flail away every time we start to dial.

Erase the Tapes in Your Mind and Let's Start Over

Before getting into the technique for making calls, I've found it truly helps salespeople to start over from the beginning. I want you to erase the tapes already playing in your mind about calling prospects. You know exactly what I'm getting at. You come to this material already predisposed against making this type of call. Many of you envision yourselves as telemarketers when it comes to sitting down for a call session. You picture the phone ringing at home just as the family sits down for dinner. You cringe seeing yourself as the scripted, droning, headset-wearing telemarketer disturbing someone with an unwanted and irrelevant intrusion. Admit it. You hate the idea of calling your target accounts because you don't want to be that person. Right? It makes you kind of queasy and, all things being equal, you'd rather take a pass.

Your Mindset Matters

What we believe makes a big difference in how we feel and how we behave. Making proactive calls to strategically selected target accounts that very likely have business issues we can address is *not* akin to telemarketing. You're not sitting in a call center with hundreds of other telemarketing reps being fed random calls from an automated dialer. You, my friend, are an important business person representing a company whose product or service potentially delivers great value to the prospect you are targeting.

When we come to the understanding that our motivation for making the call is rooted in the fact that we can probably help the prospect, everything changes. And that should certainly help change our mindset toward proactive calling. Once we view ourselves as professional problem solvers, this perspective should make us *want* to call target customers, particularly if we believe the customer will be better off working with us than someone else.

Your Voice Tone and Approach Matters, Too

It's much easier to sound great on the phone when we have a proper attitude about proactive calling. In fact, it's impossible to come off in an attractive manner when we're a bundle of nerves, tongue-tied, and clearly uncomfortable with what we're doing. I'm continually intrigued that the very same reps who thrive when dealing with existing customers completely lock up when forced to initiate phone contact with a prospective customer.

What I'm about to write seems patently obvious and unnecessary, but based on personal observation of hundreds of salespeople, it cannot be assumed: How you sound is really important during a phone call! I probably won't win an award for that thought, but it's easy to forget that buyers instantly form opinions about you and your company based on the sound of your voice. Whether that's fair or not is irrelevant. It's reality. The person you're calling cannot see your facial expressions, body language, expensive shirt, shined shoes, fancy car, or family pictures on your desk. All the other person processes is the way you sound and what your first few words communicate.

The problem with most salespeople on the phone is simple: They sound like salespeople. For some inexplicable reason, a whole lot of perfectly capable reps create a "sales voice" when speaking with potential customers. I know you've experienced this phenomenon. You're very likable, easy-to-be-around colleague who's a great conversationalist turns on this bizarre sales voice and sounds like a complete dork the moment he picks up the phone. Who taught people this trick? Where's the evidence that altering your voice to sound "salesy" is effective? Frankly, it's ridiculous, and it's hurting, not helping, us.

Do yourself a favor. Have a few trusted friends or peers listen to your calls when you're not aware they're doing it. Ask them to be blunt and tell you if you speak and sound differently making calls than you do when you're talking to peers. If that's the case, lose the sales voice. Your effectiveness will immediately increase.

I ask salespeople to use a casual, comfortable tone and to attempt to sound as normal and genuine as possible when phoning prospects. It's even helpful to be slightly informal. Remember, you're the important business person reaching out to someone who might truly benefit from visiting with you. If that's true, then you must believe it and sound like it.

It's common to hear sales reps come off as overly respectful and formal when proactively calling new prospects. I don't believe it's helpful and, frankly, believe that posture is part of what contributes to the contrived sales voice. When we're too formal and too respectful, it isn't natural. And worse, it positions us as subservient to the prospect or even conveys that we may be intimidated. I want salespeople to see themselves as equals to the buyer, and one of the best ways to accomplish that is to speak as naturally as possible.

Some of my clients are troubled by my suggestion, misinterpreting my counsel as permission to be unprofessional or disrespectful. In no way am I suggesting that. Be respectful and professional, but do it in such a way that you sound like yourself. Keep in mind that we're trying to earn a next conversation with our prospects. Do you think they will view you as someone who can bring value if you speak to them as if they're on a pedestal? I think not.

Script or No Script?

This is a biggie and generally one of the first questions I get asked. Should you use a script? No and yes.

Similar to why I don't use the term "cold call" because of the negative feelings it conjures up, I don't like the message sent by the word "script." When I hear script, I think theater and memorization. Or I mentally hear someone reading to me. And what they're reading is usually long, canned, manipulative, and obviously something they didn't write themselves. So I'm not a fan of call scripts. Most reps cannot carry off a script well, and reading to a prospect defeats all of what I just shared (in the previous sections) about mindset and voice tone.

However, I am a big proponent of call outlines and scripted talking points. Our calls should be logically structured, and we absolutely should have several key talking points scripted verbatim. Consistency matters. How can we judge what's working and what's not if we change the flow or make up new lines with every call? Especially because we worked so hard in the last chapter to craft a compelling sales story, it's imperative that we nail certain phrases dead on during introductory calls to a prospect.

Why Are We Calling? Laser Focus on the Objective

Before getting into the flow of the call and outlining techniques to be more successful, it's necessary to answer a defining question: Why are we making this call?

It sounds rudimentary, but a lot of salespeople pick up the phone without clarity on their objective. To properly conduct the call we must know exactly why we're calling this prospect. It's imperative to remain laser focused on the objective, because the prospect will likely put up defenses that we must circumvent. If we're unsure of where we'd like to end up, there's a good chance we'll get lost along the way. When locked-in firmly on the goal of the call, we're able to maneuver around the defense to redirect the conversation toward the objective.

So what's the goal of your call? I hear quite a variety of answers, but I personally believe there are only two legitimate objectives. For the inside salesperson, the goal of the proactive call is to have the full sales conversation. Inside reps are looking to set the stage for the "sales call," where they structure a dialogue with the prospect. That may happen right there on that initial phone call or it could be scheduled for a later time. I cover the flow and steps of the sales call in Chapter 11.

For the outside rep, there's simply one true objective: Get the face-to-face meeting with your target account. I tend to get a fair amount of push-back from this blanket declaration. "Aren't we supposed to qualify? If we set up too many appointments with unqualified prospects we will be wasting precious selling time. Shouldn't I try to have as thorough a conversation as possible while I have them on the phone?"

Stop Overqualifying

My resolute answer to each of those questions is no. Get the meeting. Stop overqualifying! That may sound heretical, but hear me out. There are plenty of sales experts preaching the merits of strictly qualifying your prospects before going to see them. Please consider this contrarian view.

One of the main reasons outside sales reps underperform at developing new business is because they're not in front of enough prospects. The math isn't working for them because there's not enough activity. Show me the sales rep that's failing because he's having too many unqualified appointments with strategically selected target accounts and I'll show you a thousand failing from a lack of activity.

Remember the framework: Select targets. Create and deploy weapons. Plan and execute the attack. Selecting targets is first for a reason: If we're proactively calling target accounts, the decision has already been made that we want to see them face-to-face. We put that account on our list for good strategic reasons. Let's not rethink that decision on the fly during a first phone call to that prospect. Therefore, the only logical objective for an outside salesperson's call is to score the appointment.

Lately I've been reminding clients that good things happen when talented salespeople sit in front of properly selected prospects who look a lot like their best customers. Until someone can demonstrate conclusive evidence that sales teams are wasting tons of money and time on unqualified appointments, I'll remain on my crusade swinging the pendulum back the other direction. Stop overqualifying. Laser focus on the objective and score that meeting.

Favorite Introductory Phrases for a Great Start

Anyone who makes proactive outbound calls will tell you the beginning of the call is by far the hardest. Those first few seconds are most critical and yet that's when we're most anxious. The prospect immediately forms a first impression. Once your prospects realize they've unknowingly answered a sales call, their automatic resistance shield gets deployed. So it's essential that we do everything possible early in the call to prevent that resistance shield from going up, or do our best to penetrate through it.

"Let me steal a minute" is an easy phrase that I prefer to use to kick-start the call. I say the prospect's first name, my name (first and last), and usually add my company name. "Hi, Fred. It's Mike Weinberg with The New Sales Coach. Let me steal a minute."

There are several reasons I recommend beginning the call this way. First, it fits my personal style. Those exact words may not fit you as well, but here's why I suggest it. It complies with my philosophy of sounding comfortable, conversational, and casual. I also like it because it's very far from the typical openings we hear all the time. It's not, "How are you today?" with the accent on "you." And it's a long way from the commonly pathetic, "Did I catch you at a good time?" or "Can I have a minute of your time?" Those are bad phrases and I urge you not to use them. First, they provide an easy opportunity for the prospect to give you an answer you don't want. But more than that, I advise against them because they are what every other salesperson says. You don't want to tip your hand and have the contact lump you in with all those other reps interrupting his day or wasting his time.

There are a few other neat benefits from saying "Let me steal a minute." I like acknowledging on the front end that I'm an unexpected intrusion. It's human and real. In a subtle way, it lets the prospect know that I get it. I'm looking to steal a minute from him, so it's just calling it what it is. Unlike the typical opening, this approach intrigues the person and creates an opportunity for the prospect to connect with you. The prospect's response also opens the door for you to demonstrate respect while scoring relationship points. If we truly caught the person at a horrendous time (on the way to a meeting with her boss or rushing to finish up a project to make the FedEx cutoff), isn't it better to let the person go? There's no rule forcing you to have the full conversation on your first attempt. When I can tell the prospect is harried and not in a state to engage me, even for a minute, I offer to let her go.

No one's happy to pick up the phone only to be ambushed by an uninvited salesperson. That type of reaction is typical. But there are times when you just sense the prospect is in a bad spot. Other trainers will suggest launching into your script since you have the person on the phone. I recommend letting the prospect go, telling (not asking) the person that you'll call back another time, and scoring the points for being human. I promise you that the second call you make to that prospect will be easier. You'll be more confident and the prospect will likely think more highly of you for being sensitive to his situation. "Hi, Fred. It's Mike Weinberg getting back with you. I'm the guy who caught you late on Tuesday trying to run out to FedEx." Pause. Let him thank you. Then proceed as two normal humans engaging in a dialogue. This works because it changes the entire dynamic and feel of the call.

"I head up..." is the next phrase out of my mouth. Before going any further, I want to position who I am in the prospect's mind. If I handled the first part well, he likely is not viewing me as the typical salesperson and there's a good shot at keeping his resistance shield down. I absolutely love the phrase "I head up" and you'll love it, too.

As important as what it may communicate to your contact is what it does for your own psyche. You're not a telemarketer or unnecessary disturbance. You're an important business person who heads up a part of your company. I want you to sound confident and comfortable and this little phrase does wonders to help you believe it. Say it out loud a few times. "I head up the western United States for ABC Company." "I head up our education business." "I head up client relationships for XYZ." "I head up our agency team." "I head up our reseller business." "I head up our southeast territory."

Some salespeople struggle saying it because they see themselves as being too low on the totem pole. I don't care what your official title may be. We can figure out a way for you to incorporate this great line into your calls. No matter your formal position, you head up something for your company. Practice saying it: "I head up…" It will make you feel good and paint you as someone the prospect should be interested in and paying attention to.

Crafting Your Telephone Mini Power Statement

So far, so good. We sat down with the right mindset, seeing ourselves as professionals who want to place that call because we can help the prospect. We used a normal conversational voice, acknowledged we were interrupting without apologizing, and have positioned ourselves as someone worthy of engaging for a brief conversation. And now we find ourselves at a moment of truth: What in the world do we say to entice the prospect to talk further and invite us in to meet face-to-face?

This is the place to surgically insert a finely tuned, miniature version of that fantastic power statement we created in the previous chapter. The goal is to serve up a killer appetizer—a delicious mouth-watering tease that creates a strong hunger for the main course, which is the face-to-face meeting we're pursuing.

When delivered properly, this telephone version of the power statement establishes exactly how we want the prospect to see us—as someone that people like him (or companies like his) look to for guidance when faced with challenging issues.

The hard work was already done; that is, you did the heavy lifting when you wrote your full-page power statement back in Chapter 8. For the mini version to be delivered over the phone, I suggest grabbing your two favorite "client issues" bullets (from the pains removed, problems solved, opportunities captured, results achieved section). I like to pick one that's unique and provocative, and another that's broad and likely applicable to almost any prospect on your list. You may also want to select one differentiator from that section of the power statement. But that's the limit: two client issues and one differentiator. Any more would take too long to say and we'd sound as if we were reading a script.

The key is using this phone power statement in a conversational manner. For instance:

Hi, Steve. It's Rob Thompson with Allsafe Security. I'm getting back with you; I caught you right in the middle of a big tenant situation a couple days ago. [Steve laughs about his crazy tenant, thanks you for your understanding, and asks what you want.]

Steve, I head up our client service team for the downtown corridor. Right now a lot of property managers are looking to Allsafe because they're faced with excessive liability exposure and growing life/safety fears for corporate tenants and guests. We're also helping a good number of management companies like yours [mention Steve's company by name] who are concerned their current security solution may no longer be adequate. [Stop.]

That is a mini power statement to deliver over the phone. It was long enough already, so I didn't want to toss in a differentiator. From what I know about Steve's company, I was pretty confident I picked two issues that are salient to him. At this point, the best thing to do is stop. Our natural instinct, which is wrong, is to keep talking and fill the silence. But because I want the prospect to process the issues I tossed out and to associate me as someone who helps people like him address those issues, I chose to leave it there. Steve will certainly respond with something, and then I have a choice. If I like what he says, I'll move ahead to the next step and ask him to visit with me. If I judge that it would be helpful to fire a differentiator at him or mention another client issue we address, then I'll do that, and then follow up by asking for the meeting. Make sense?

For the Inside Rep: Build a Bridge

This section is for the inside salesperson only. The outside rep has served the appetizer and should move on by inviting the prospect to join him for the main course (see the next section). That meal generally gets scheduled in the future at the prospect's place of business. The inside rep, however, has more work to do on this initial call.

I spent a lot of time this past year working with inside sales teams. Anecdotal evidence suggests that the number of inside sales teams is increasing as companies look to be more efficient and also better understand how to cover the market from within their own offices. I believe technology and the desire to reduce selling expenses will continue to drive increasing numbers of inside sales roles. Hear me clearly: Inside sales is not a second-class job. I've learned a ton from working with some outstanding professionals. My former employee and friend Roy is the best I've seen. He happily shares best practices with me and has helped shape my coaching content. Roy takes it as a personal challenge to outsell the outside reps at his company. He does it quarter after quarter. I know because he forwards me the sales reports!

After delivering the telephone power statement, the inside rep needs to build a bridge to the sales conversation. Depending on the prospect's willingness to engage, the easiest thing to do is to begin a dialogue by following the power statement with simple probing questions. It can also be highly effective to share relevant information you discovered doing precall research. You can directly ask the prospect how to go about building a meaningful relationship with the company. It's amazing what guidance people will offer when you ask for help (assuming the person you're speaking with is not the brother-in-law of the competitor you're trying to supplant).

The most beneficial thing the inside rep can do is listen. Work hard to learn about the prospect's current situation and record helpful information that will be useful as you continue working the account, seeking to uncover opportunities.

Ask for the Meeting, Ask Again, and Once More

This is, by far, my favorite part of the proactive call. It's why we called in the first place. After delivering the mini power statement, ask the contact for the meeting. Unless you believe you have no choice because the prospect insists on vetting you further on the phone, keep your eye squarely on the prize and ask for the meeting.

Here's the secret: Be ready to ask three times. You read that right. Three times. You've got to be willing to push past resistance. Even if you executed perfectly, from voice tone to articulating the client issues you solve, there's an incredibly high likelihood that the prospect will say no to your request. In other words, it's not your fault. It's nothing you did or did not do. The prospect is programmed to say no. It's automatic. Moron salespeople ruined it for us. Buyers are so busy and so fed up with salespeople wasting their time that, no matter how great you sound, their first answer is usually no. So don't take it personally. But don't hang up the phone, either.

This is one of the reasons highly relational people who intensely dislike conflict have a hard time with prospecting. Prospecting involves conflict and pushing past resistance. Too often salespeople will state that they don't want to come off as pushy. I understand. But I'm telling you now, this is one of those times that we've got to push. If you cave at this point, thank the prospect for her time and hang up, you fail. And you'll continue to fail.

Many client reps come back to me after coaching to brag about the success they're having on the phone. Consistently, they credit it to their new willingness to ask three separate times for the meeting. I wish they were telling me about my brilliant call outline or power statement formula. But what they share aligns with my personal experience: It's on the third ask, usually, that the prospect relents and invites us in. Let me provide some ideas and magic words to help you make the most of your three asks.

Three Magic Words

There are three *magic words* I use over and over and over when making proactive telephone calls. These words work, and I encourage you to incorporate them into every request for a meeting. The three words are *visit, fit,* and *value.*

1. *Visit.* I like to ask the prospect to visit with me. "Appointment" sounds so clinical, and no one is sitting around wishing for another meeting to attend. "Visit" is a positive word. You visit with family and friends. "I'd like to *visit with you...*" or "Would you have thirty minutes to *visit with me* next Tuesday or Wednesday?"

2. *Fit.* "Fit" is one of my overall favorite sales words. It demonstrates confidence and also disarms the prospect. It's nonthreatening and shows you're not desperate. "Let's get together to see *if we might be a fit* to help you..." or "I'd like to learn more about your situation, share how we're helping XYZ organizations like yours, and determine together *if there's enough of a fit* to talk about a next step."

3. *Value.* Value is what everyone is talking about and seems to be the yardstick by which we are all measured today. I suggest using the word in a couple of ways. One way is: "We'll review your current situation and see if *we can bring some value* to what you're doing..." The other way is to promise prospects that they'll receive value from the meeting, which is part of the enticement to invite you in. That usually happens after a prospect has predictably said "no" to the first and second requests for the meeting. Then it's time to put together the trifecta and use all three magic words in combination: "Judy, I understand that you're [insert her objection here]. *Visit with me* anyway. I promise *you'll get value* and ideas from our time together, even if we end up not *being a fit* to help you."

Winning with Voice Mail

Voice mail is a fact of life. If we're making proactive telephone calls, then we're going to get our contact's voice mail. Based on polling I've done with my clients, it appears reps end up in voice mail almost three-quarters of the time. That's a big number. Back in the day (what does that mean, anyway?), I would make several attempts before leaving a voice mail for a prospect. But when only one of four calls connects with a live contact, we need to take full advantage of the opportunity voice mail presents.

Here are six thoughts on how you can win with voice mail:

1. *Adopt a positive perspective.* Most people making a living in sales complain about voice mail. They dread it. And it kills their energy, enthusiasm, and effectiveness. Stop the whining and start seeing the opportunity it provides to "touch" the prospect. We all know it takes X number of touches to break through. Be thankful for the chance to make this a positive touch.

2. *Expect and prepare for it.* I'm a master at babbling like an idiot on someone's voice mail. We've all done it. We've puked out non-sense. We've gone on too long. We've talked in circles. We've panicked and starting hitting the pound key or the star key hoping to kill the evidence of our pathetic effort. If we're going to get voice mail three-quarters of time, shouldn't we begin to expect it? Be prepared to leave a well-crafted articulate message.

3. *Use a snippet of your story.* Go ahead and make it a productive message. Similar to our mini telephone power statement, leave a tiny piece of your story. Pick one or two main client issues. Don't ramble. Think how you react to long, drawn-out, repetitive messages. We want to leave them intrigued to hear more.

4. *Take the long view; see it as a campaign.* Accept that it's going to take multiple messages to get a call back. Picture this particular

voice mail message as one in a series. That will help keep it succinct and prevent you from leaving ninety-second messages. Add a touch of variety using a different snippet of your sales story with each message. The reality is that almost nobody calls back after receiving one message from a salesperson. So plan to make it a campaign.

5. *Ask for a call back; state that you will call again.* Yes, leave your number at a pace that gives the prospect time to actually write it down and ask to be called back. But make sure to let them know that you'll call again. We want to send the message that we're serious about reaching them. When I receive e-mails or voice mails from a salesperson, I like to test them to see if they're serious about pursuing me. I almost never respond to the first attempt. It's shocking how few ever make a second attempt to get me. It communicates that I must not be a high priority. Don't be a "one and done" salesperson.

6. *Be human. Use humor or guilt, not anger.* One of the keys to telephone prospecting is to convert the buyer from seeing you an anonymous salesperson making robocalls to viewing you as a real-life human being. To make that happen through voice mail, we need to sound and act like real people, normal people with feelings. For whatever reason, salespeople are not viewed as real people when making proactive calls. Prospects don't respond to robots going through the motions. They're much more likely to respond to a fellow member of humanity who has a great story and is making a supreme effort to pique their interest. If I haven't received a return call after a few messages it's time to ramp up the human side. I like to do that with humor and possibly a little guilt thrown in. It's amazing how often the return call finally comes after a third message that includes something funny or plays on the fact that "I hope by now I've earned a callback based on perseverance alone." Similar to asking three times for the meeting, somehow the third

voice mail tends to do the trick. Also, never get angry or show frustration in a message. We have no right to be angry at prospects who don't know us and haven't asked us to call. If they're not calling back, it's on us, not on them.

The telephone can be an effective friend and critical part of our new business development attack. But your friendship with the phone requires an investment on your part. The phone gets a bad rap because salespeople cannot use it effectively or will not use it at all. It's up to you. My encouragement is to try the techniques I've outlined throughout this chapter. There's no way to improve your proactive telephone skills without practice. Confidence will lead to success, and more success will increase your confidence. To practice, start by calling smaller or more insignificant accounts. As you get more comfortable with this methodology, you'll find yourself opening doors you never thought possible.

Questions for Reflection

➤ What negative feelings or baggage have you been bringing to your proactive calling sessions?

➤ How have you been preparing to make calls, and what additions should you make to your standard preparations?

➤ Do you see yourself as an important business person calling your prospects because you might be able to help them? If not, what can you do to change your mindset about making calls?

➤ If scoring the appointment is the clear objective, how should that affect the way you structure the call?

➤ When will you carve out the time to work on creating your mini phone power statement?

CHAPTER 10

Mentally Preparing for the Face-to-Face Sales Call

To me, the initial face-to-face call with a target prospect is the pinnacle of what we do as sales professionals. Securing this meeting is the focus of all our hard work up to this point. Sure, there can be a ton of work following that first meeting, and it might be months or even years until a deal is consummated, depending on the sales cycle. Some people will argue the boardroom presentation is our finest moment, while others believe that the formal proposal is the summit of the sales effort. My experience shows that business is won earlier in the process by those who get in front of declared target accounts and set the tone for the relationship during sales calls.

It's Your Call; You Need a Plan

Make no mistake about it. It's *your* sales call. Even when the prospect pursues you and requests a meeting, it is your call. In the next chapter, we'll review, in great detail, an easy and potent way to share your agenda, establish ownership of the meeting, and come across as a total professional to your contact.

Previously I mentioned that good things happen when a talented salesperson gets face-to-face with a target prospect. The converse is that bad things tend to happen when the salesperson doesn't have a plan for the meeting. Most outside reps are pretty good about having a clear goal for their calls, but equally as bad about having a formalized plan for how the meeting should flow.

Not long ago I was working in the field with a client rep. I won't name the city to protect the guilty. Before jumping out of the car to call on a significant account, I asked a pretty standard set of questions for which the salesperson had decent answers: "Tell me about the people we are meeting. Why do they think we are here today and what are they expecting? What is a win for us?"

I then asked one more question—and received quite a memorable answer. "What is your plan for the call?" I asked. The rep shared that he doesn't like to plan out his calls because that comes off as mechanical. "Oh," I replied. "Well, tell me how this is gonna go down, then?" The salesperson answered that he prefers his meetings to be *organic*. I was amused at the application of this overused word and figured I was in for an adventure.

What transpired was predictable. I never felt comfortable the entire meeting. The sales rep did not find a groove. It was organic alright, vacillating between the buyer controlling the meeting (since we did not attempt to) and the buyer sitting quietly while the salesperson babbled on nervously in front of me. If I had known this rep better or worked with this client longer, I probably would have thrown him a life preserver by interjecting a few pain- or opportunity-seeking questions. But I refrained and experienced the agony of defeat along with my client. And honestly, the benefit from this coaching opportunity outweighed the failure of this one call.

That lovely organic experience heightened my awareness of the widespread nature of this issue across sales teams today. Very few salespeople at small and midsize companies are being mentored on the basic fundamentals of sales. I began asking every sales leader and rep how they were planning for and conducting sales calls. What I heard was not pretty.

Kicking off a coaching session for a team of five seasoned reps at an old-school manufacturing company, I asked them to share the last time someone reviewed how to structure a sales call. Zero out of five could answer. I dug deeper to discover that none of them *ever* had a manager, coach, or trainer model how to plan a sales call before. And these were veteran salespeople, not rookies. Frightening.

That same week I was meeting one-on-one with producers at a first-rate insurance agency. One producer was heading out for a full week on the road to renew several clients and meet with a couple of large potential accounts. We talked through her strategy and sales story talking points (which were excellent), and I inquired about her thoughts for structuring these meetings. After pausing for a moment, the producer admitted it had been a long time since she was challenged to visualize and plan the flow of a sales call. We dug in together and thirty minutes later, she had a clear structure and agenda for both client and prospect meetings. That Friday she left me the most thankful voice mail message sharing how confident and in control she felt going into those calls with a plan.

Avoid Defaulting to the Buyer's Process

Said simply, if we don't have a plan and process when sitting down with a prospect, then the meeting will default to the buyer's process. Keep in mind that our potential customers are accustomed to suffering through poorly run sales calls. That's the norm. And they are tired of salespeople wasting their precious time.

We've got to walk in prepared to lay out our own plan for the call. If we don't, expect the prospect to quickly jump in the driver's seat and you'll be the one taken on a ride. How often have you seen a sales call begin with the prospect asking, "What do you have for me?" Salespeople are completely thrown for a loop by the buyer who starts things off by saying, "You've got your thirty minutes. Go." They usually go alright, all over themselves. Even worse is the aggressive prospect who goes on the offensive, peppering you with question after question right from the outset. Before catching your breath, you're back on your heels being led down paths you didn't intend to travel. Thirty minutes later you're still playing defense and haven't learned the first thing yet about the buyer or his situation. Not good.

Bring a Pad and Pen; Please Leave the Projector at Home

"Presenting" is not a synonym for "selling." Just because you can build a slick PowerPoint presentation doesn't mean you should. It would take an incredibly strong argument and unique set of circumstances to convince me why anyone would need a projector for an initial meeting with a prospect.

Recently I was contacted by a company referred by a client of mine. It's always nice when a potential customer pursues you. We set up a meeting, and I could tell right away the company had some big sales problems. I walked in the room and the entire senior management team was seated at the conference table. I worked my way around the room, shaking hands and repeating the name of each person I met. The younger guy in charge of sales looked surprised that I wasn't setting up any equipment. In a concerned voice he asked if I had everything I needed for my presentation. I smiled, debating with myself whether to give a smartass answer. Choosing to be respectful, I simply said yes, opened my notebook, and pulled out an expensive-looking pen. I did have a one-page handout that provides an overview to my coaching framework, but that remains tucked in a folder until I gather the information needed to connect my approach to the company's issues.

For the life of me, I cannot figure why salespeople see initial meetings as opportunities to present a capabilities overview. I hear it all the time. "They've asked us to come in and do a capabilities overview. Let's pull together our best stuff." Huh?

New business development success results from creating a sales dialogue, not perfecting a monologue. One of my sales laws is that discovery always precedes presentation. Always. It's sales malpractice when it doesn't. Pitchmen and product-pushers present before they fully understand the customer's situation. Consultative sales professionals gather information, connect with the prospect, and begin building a relationship before presenting solutions.

Years ago, my former partner Donnie and I were leading a client's national sales team meeting and sharing perspective on conducting sales calls. We were having fun and teasing the reps who had fallen in love with the sound of their own voices. To drive home the message, we had the team share horrific examples of what we called the "show up and throw up" sales move. One of the young stars in the room yelled out that he had a better name for it. He called it the "spray and pray" approach. The salesperson goes first and just sprays out everything he can to the prospect. Then he prays he hit on something relevant. Perfect.

Stop confusing presenting with selling! At initial sales calls, I'm betting on the sales pro with the pad and pen defeating the pitchman with the projector every time.

God Gave You Two Ears and One Mouth

Newsflash: Salespeople like to talk. Unfortunately, most of us talk a disproportionate amount of time when in front of a customer. When joining reps on calls I like to track the percentage of time the salesperson talks versus the amount the buyer talks. After the meeting we debrief and I ask a handful of questions to get the rep's assessment of the call. Then I ask about the rep's talk-listen ratio. The salesperson usually admits that he should have asked more questions, but feels good about the balance. The results are often mind-blowing when the salesperson learns he spoke 80 percent to 90 percent of the words during the meeting.

One of the most memorable sales lessons came early in my career.

I was the traveling assistant to Danny Abraham, the founder and CEO of Slim-Fast Foods. Danny was the ultimate marketeer and consummate salesman. He was in his mid-sixties and very much at the helm of the company as it became one of the hottest brands in the country. I was fortunate to spend two years as his assistant, attending everything from TV commercial shoots with celebrities to late-night dinners with Dodgers' manager Tommy Lasorda. When Danny tired of chartering private jets, he entrusted me with the task of buying his first Gulfstream. Let's just say it was a cherry assignment. Nothing was more fun than christening the plane by pouring a can of Slim-Fast over the nose cone.

While running the flight department and flying in the jump seat were the glamorous parts of the job, the real-life MBA education came from sitting beside Danny in meetings with major suppliers and customers. We would regularly head out for cross-country trips that included seeing key accounts such as Walgreens, Target, and Albertsons in the same week.

Danny loved to sell, and he was extremely critical of how the sales force would represent the company and our products, which he considered his babies. It was quite a scene when we would show up in a regional sales manager's territory to call on an account. The nervous local sales manager would meet us at the airport with new product samples, milk on ice, and blender in tow. The local manager, the vice president of sales, Danny, and I would pile into the back of the limo and head to the customer's buying office. You could tell the sales manager was keyed up and anxious to *present* our new flavors and line extensions in front of Danny and the merchandise team at the account.

My memorable lesson came on a particular trip to Minnesota to meet with Target at a time when Wal-Mart was cleaning everyone's clock in the health and beauty aids category. This was billed as a critical meeting with very senior people at Target. The sales manager in Minneapolis was named Keith, and it was obvious how well prepared he was for the big meeting. He executed what seemed like a perfect presentation of our programs and products, and you could tell he was pleased with the meeting. On the limo ride back to the airport, Danny was kinder than usual in his evaluation of the meeting. But then he leaned forward and put a hand on Keith's knee.

I can hear Danny's voice every time I retell this story. "Keith, you did a nice job today with our products. Thank you for the care you put into the presentation. But you talked too much. We didn't learn what we should have about their business. God gave you two ears and one mouth for a reason, and that's the percent you should use them. When you're talking you aren't learning. Two ears, one mouth. Remember that for next time."

Today, Danny is a billionaire after selling the company to Unilever. He knew a thing or two about sales. I'm thankful for the opportunity he provided and the invaluable education I received. Twenty-two years later, I still share that lesson with every salesperson who will listen.

Selling from the Same Side of the Table

It has always bothered me that the seller-buyer relationship is set up as adversarial. Why do sales calls feel unnatural? How come we can sense tension in the room? That's not how it's supposed to be. Is it?

But what if your prospects sensed that you were on their side of the table? If you had their best interest at heart and were working to see the world through their eyes? What would be different in the dynamic of the sales call if you approached the prospect as an ally and created an environment where it was natural to dialogue *with* the buyer instead of talking *at* the buyer?

I ask salespeople to do everything possible to create a selling environment where it feels like we're on the same side of the table as the buyer—figuratively and literally. Why do most people choose to sit on opposite sides of the table during a sales call? That doesn't make sense. It sends the wrong message and perpetuates the adversarial dynamic we should be working to change. I understand it can be weird to sit down right next to the person, especially when it's only the two of you at a rectangular table. So sit perpendicular to the buyer at a ninety-degree angle. It's not as odd as it sounds, and it creates a completely different aura than sitting opposite the person. (At a round table, you can absolutely sit down next to someone without it being awkward.) I don't want to start the relationship feeling like we're opposed to each other. Before sitting down, especially in a very large room, take a second to decide the best way to physically communicate that you are there as an ally, not an adversary.

Questions for Reflection

► In what ways have you been guilty of ceding control of the sales call to the buyer?

► How dependent have you become on your projector?

► How might you handle the prospect who is expecting your dog and pony show during the initial meeting?

► Reflect on your standard talk-listen ratio. How difficult would it be to move toward one-third talking, two-thirds listening? What would have to change?

► How might you differently position yourself, physically and verbally, to come across as more of an ally than an adversary during sales calls?

CHAPTER 11

Structuring Winning Sales Calls

We don't go on sales calls. We conduct them. The professional sales-person isn't riding along in the back of an airplane. She's in the left seat, up in the cockpit, with her left hand on the yoke, right hand on the throttles, and feet on the rudder pedals. Think pilot-in-command. There's nothing passive about it.

A flight has a proper and logical sequence of events. We check the weather, file a flight plan, and do a preflight inspection of the plane. We run through a checklist on the ground, start the engine, and scan the vital instruments. We decide when it's time to taxi away and then request permission to take the runway. From there we execute the remaining segments of the flight: takeoff, climb out, cruise, descent, approach, and landing. A properly structured sales call has a similar flow and number of stages. And the order of the stages has a significant effect on the outcome of the call or flight.

Structuring the sales call properly greatly enhances our chances of winning. Because most salespeople do not structure their calls well, it's a wonderful opportunity to differentiate ourselves. Well-structured calls help us begin the relationship with the prospect on the right foot and position ourselves exactly how we'd like to be seen. We're also able to maintain control of the call because it's clear to the buyer we have a plan. Once we share and get buy-in on the proposed agenda, most prospects gladly let us fly the plane because they're relieved to be in the hands of a competent sales pilot. A solid plan also protects us from talking too much or selling too soon during the meeting.

The Phases of a Winning Sales Call

There are seven phases for the call with a prospect and eight for an existing customer.

1. Build rapport and identify the buyer's style.

2. Share the agenda (get buy-in, seek input).

3. Clean up their issues (only with existing customers).

4. Deliver the power statement (three minutes maximum).

5. Ask probing questions (also known as discovery).

6. Sell.

7. Determine the fit and seek out objections.

8. Define and schedule the next steps.

Build Rapport and Identify the Buyer's Style

This first important phase of the call is to help us connect with the buyer. There are many theories about when or if rapport building should be part of the sales call today. I think it's critical. Some people suggest small talk is archaic; we should skip it completely and get on to business. Other gurus proclaim that we should definitely build rapport, but not until the end of the meeting.

I have two goals for this first phase of the call. First and foremost, I want to make the prospect comfortable. I want to connect relationally, if at all possible. I don't mean pointing at the giant marlin mounted on the wall, asking if the buyer likes to fish, or commenting on the beautiful family picture on the credenza. That's an old-school stereotype, and cheesy. I mean that you can potentially talk about the day's news headline, or last night's sports team victory, or you can mention something intriguing from the prospect's LinkedIn profile.

Salespeople always ask how much time they should spend building rapport. There's only one correct answer and you'll agree it makes a lot of sense: Rapport building should last as long as the person you are meeting wants it to last! The sales call is not about us, and this is our first opportunity to demonstrate we understand that. If we're visiting with a chatty relational type who keeps asking personal questions or wants to spend a half-hour reliving his night at the ballgame, go with it. But if you sense the contact is a hard-charging business driver who's giving one-word answers to your friendly questions, move forward to the next phase of the call. Quickly.

The other objective of spending time to build rapport is to figure out who you have in front of you. Is this a reserved, quiet, analytical person who speaks at half my volume and one-fourth the speed I do? Or is this a happy-go-lucky executive whose passion is to experience life to the fullest and who just wants to feel good? Maybe you're sitting across from a competitive, driven, conflict-loving, bottom-line executive. Whatever the case, we can learn a lot about the behavioral style of the buyer in a minute or two.

The key is to get a basic handle on the other person's style so that you can prepare to adapt your style as the call progresses. My cheat sheet coaching on this topic is simple yet very helpful. Slightly adapt your approach to be more like the customer. Smile to make the happy buyer feel good. Speed up and push hard with the hard-charger. Slow down and be ready to provide details for the analytical type. Some trainers use the term "mirroring" to describe the methodology of copying the buyer's style. I don't like asking salespeople to "act," so

I'm not a fan of the term. However, the concept is on target. Adapting our approach allows the buyer to "hear" what we're saying because we're communicating in a behavioral language that makes the prospect comfortable.

When we feel the buyer is ready to move beyond rapport building, we transition to sharing our agenda and setting up the call.

Share the Agenda and Set up the Call

This is *the most important* phase of the sales call. Sharing your agenda and setting up the call is your best opportunity to set the tone for the meeting and demonstrate the meeting will be a valuable and different experience for your contact. Letting the prospect in on your plan produces three meaningful benefits:

1. *It is a big differentiator.* Almost no one in sales does this. Certainly not well. Letting your prospect in on your plan communicates that you aren't an amateur, that you've done this before and you respect the time the prospect has allotted to you. After laying out your plan for the meeting, you can also reinforce once again that this meeting isn't about you but about the prospect. You do that by asking a smart question: "That is what I was looking to do in our time together. What would you like to get from this meeting; what were you hoping to accomplish today?" Depending on the person and how difficult it was to secure the meeting, I sometimes add a bold twist: "Why did you invite me in?" Or, "I was just curious. How come you agreed to visit with me?" Try it. You'll be pleasantly surprised by the effect.

2. *It informs the buyer where you are headed.* No one wants to be taken on a ride. I can't stand not knowing where I'm going. Whether it's a road trip or meeting conducted by someone else, I get real antsy when I don't know where things are headed.

Sharing your agenda provides the buyer with a road map for the meeting. It is a professional courtesy that, in most cases, makes the person you're meeting feel more comfortable.

3. *It lets the buyer know you expect a dialogue.* Your prospect fully expects you to pull the usual "show up and throw up" act that he has become accustomed to. He's thinking, "I don't need to play close attention because you are about to verbally puke on me for the next hour." In many cases, as soon as the salesperson opens her mouth the buyer lapses into selective listening mode, fully expecting the call to be a monologue. Powerfully sharing your agenda actually shakes things up for the buyer. Your goal here is to shock the prospect by surprising him with your solid plan, and that you are expecting to engage in a dialogue.

Since so few salespeople properly set up the call, most haven't benefited from observing it done well. My clients appreciate when it is spelled out with an example. When running my own sales calls, here is how I transition from rapport building to sharing the agenda:

Ron, thanks for inviting me in. I believe we set up this meeting for thirty minutes. How are you on time? [Pause for an answer.] Great. I will make sure we are done before 11:30.

Here's what I would like to do. Let me kick us off and take just two or three minutes to share a bit about ABC Spellbinders, the issues we solve for HR professionals, and why they tend to bring us in for help. I will also touch briefly on how we are different and why we have been so successful in this space. Then I'd like to turn the tables and ask you questions to understand more about your situation and what you are doing in regards to QRS, or how you are approaching the XYZ opportunity. Depending on what I hear from you, I can share a few relevant case studies or show you options for how we provide Spellbinding for clients. After that, we can discuss if it looks like we might be a fit to help you or if there is a logical next step [such as whether it makes sense to have a follow-up meeting or get our teams together].

That is what I was hoping to do, Ron. Tell me what you were hoping for and what you would like to walk away with today.

Every single phrase in this sample opening is intentional. If this is a completely new concept for you, my challenge is to take the time and dissect this example piece by piece. Think about how you have been (or haven't been) setting up your own sales calls and what that communicates to your prospects.

Sharing your agenda to set up the call is an incredible opportunity to position yourself and your company. I strongly encourage you to invest the time and energy to master this technique.

Clean Up Their Issues

Obviously, this phase of the call only applies when meeting with an existing customer. (We would certainly hope that a company we have yet to do business with doesn't have complaints or issues with us!) I shared this concept with the designer who helps put together my coaching content and presentation materials. He calls this important step "dealing with the junk up front." That pretty much says it all.

If my lovely wife is frustrated from a bad interaction with me earlier in the day, it's safe to say she isn't too interested in hearing about my exciting news or the great progress I made for a client. It doesn't matter what I want to talk about because her mind is still processing the displeasure I created previously.

It's the same with customers. If we want to accomplish something productive on a sales call, it's imperative that we clean up their issues before moving ahead with what we want to achieve. Clear the air. Attempting to show your preoccupied customers great new products while they're still seething about a missed shipment, unfulfilled promise, or poor service experience is fruitless. They can't hear you until you deal with what's on their mind.

Deliver the Power Statement

For all the uses and great versatility of the power statement, this phase of the sales call is when it delivers maximum impact. Here we deploy the full-form power statement in all of its glory. In phone calls, voice mails, e-mails, and other sales weapons we're limited to using bits and pieces of our power statement, but at this point in the meeting we can let it fly.

In three enrapturing minutes of sales magnificence we deliver the prospect a succinct, compelling, client-focused understanding of why people or companies come to us, what we offer, and how we are different from, and better than, other alternatives. When executed properly it's a thing of beauty that brings a tear to my eyes. More important, it works wonders on the prospect.

With neither projector nor brochure, but with eloquence and great power, you put forth your story and engage the mind of the prospect in a way most salespeople never will.

Pay careful attention to the customer's physical reactions while you're walking through your power statement, particularly the first segment where you explain the issues, pains, and problems addressed, along with the results you achieve for clients. Very often customers will react when you hit on a salient issue. Look for a wince, a nod, or even a hand gesture acknowledging that you pushed an important button. If someone starts writing feverishly, smile on the inside knowing you're on to something good! It's not unusual for your potential customer to interrupt you to ask a clarifying question or for more details about one of your client issues. Provide a clear, brief answer to the question, but stop yourself from launching into a full-blown sales pitch. Remember the flight analogy? There's a time to climb, a time to cruise at altitude, and a time to land. It takes discipline because our sales instinct wants to pounce on the opening. Be patient and keep your powder dry. Make note of what aroused the customer's interest so that you can explore the cause during the next stage of the call.

Let's pause and review where you are in the meeting. At this point, you are likely somewhere between seven and fifteen minutes into the call. You're in complete control and the potential buyer is thankful and surprised by this unique and engaging experience. You've gained relational ground by following the prospect's lead in building rapport for an appropriate amount of time. You've assessed the buyer's style and are making slight adaptations to your delivery (e.g., the speed and volume of your voice, your body language) in order to improve communication. You've masterfully shared a well-thought-out plan for the call and sought the buyer's input and buy-in. The buyer now sees you are a professional and is comfortable letting you lead. He has also been put on alert that you expect him to engage in a dialogue and that you aren't going to present at him for the next hour. If meeting with an existing account, you've demonstrated that the customer's issues are a priority by doing some housekeeping to clean up outstanding items. Then, in a very compressed manner, you've shared your story, providing a list of reasons other people turn to you for help, what your company sells, and why you are the best choice. Wow, not a bad ten or so minutes. Wouldn't you agree?

Before moving ahead to the next phase of your call, I'd like to address a question often posed by experienced sales reps about the prospect's willingness to answer questions. A good number of salespeople aren't comfortable leading a dialogue with a potential customer. They like to talk, pitch, and present because that feels familiar to them, but some are also afraid the customer won't respond well to their questions. Beyond that, some sellers are concerned the customer will be reluctant to provide information and could take offense at being interrogated (sales reps' biased words, not mine). These reps argue that we should first give our full presentation, thereby earning the right to question the prospect.

I use two responses to help alter the doubting salesperson's perspective. First, let's not view the prospect as a witness facing hostile cross-examination. Is it not more accurate to see yourself as the doctor and your potential customer as the patient looking to cure an ill or achieve a health breakthrough? You wouldn't trust a physician who walked into the examining room, spent an hour telling you how great he was, and then wrote a prescription, would you? The same concept applies to the sales process. Discovery precedes presentation.

This is where the power statement pays huge dividends. You share enough meaningful information on the front end to build credibility, create interest, and help the prospect warm up to answering important questions. This is analogous to meeting your new doctor. This time your new doc sits down on that rolling stool, engages you in small talk, then gives a three-minute overview of her education, specialty, and philosophy of care. You now believe she's competent and are more receptive to being examined and answering questions about your health. Following the examination, the doc shares her thoughts, diagnoses your condition, and suggests a solution. That's a great example of how to best structure your sales calls.

Ask Probing Questions: Discovery

When we were little they taught us that there's no such thing as a stupid question. They lied. Salespeople are notorious for asking obvious, ignorant, and off-target questions.

More selling can be accomplished by asking a series of great questions than by executing a highly polished presentation. The operative word here is *great*. The skilled sales hunter uses this phase of the call to ask targeted, probing questions to demonstrate expertise, identify potential opportunities, gather necessary information, and move the ball forward.

There are dozens of books and even entire selling systems devoted to schooling sales professionals on probing methodology. There's enough material out there to earn a doctorate degree on the topic. We won't go that deep here, but I will offer a simple framework to group probing questions into four categories that ensure we discover the information we need:

1. Personal questions

2. Strategic and directional questions

3. Specific issue-seeking and opportunity-seeking questions

4. Sales process questions

Personal Questions

The old adage says that people buy from people they like. I couldn't agree more, and there's no better way to earn people's affection than to help them get what they want. That means asking questions to discover what personally matters to your prospects. What are their short- and long-term goals? How are they being evaluated? What type of results are they working to achieve? How could you make their life easier? How and when do they get bonuses or promoted?

Sure, some of these questions are deeply personal and may not be appropriate in all circumstances. But be open to the concept of working hard to understand what is personally important to your potential customer. The deepest and most successful client relationships result when there's mutual trust and personal commitment between buyer and seller. Isn't that the type of long-term partnership we desire?

Strategic and Directional Questions

These questions help us get a handle on what is taking place in the prospect's macro world. What's going on in your customers' space? Who are they up against in the market? What industry trends are working for or against their situation? Are there corporate initiatives or new strategies catalyzing change? Is there pressure to grow and expand or to reduce costs?

Precall research can aid you in framing these questions so that they're more specific rather than generic. There is no excuse for making a business-to-business sales call without having fully investigated your prospect using all available means. At a minimum, scan publicly available information, press releases, social media sites, and anything senior executives or your contact have said or written lately. How smart will you look to your prospect when asking questions about a speech their chief marketing officer made last week that you discovered on YouTube? Or how unprepared or lazy will you sound asking questions that have readily available answers? In the latter case, you'll only prove that you didn't care enough to do your homework.

Specific Issue- and Opportunity-Seeking Questions

Once you become more familiar with your prospect's big-picture world, it's time to probe more specifically into areas where your offerings can make a difference. Your objective is to gather every morsel of information to identify if and how you can help this prospect.

The easiest way to formulate effective questions is to review the client issues section of your power statement (problems solved, pains removed, opportunities captured, results achieved). Work through the entire list, taking each of the stated reasons that clients look to your company and converting it into a probing question. It's helpful to keep the questions open-ended because this encourages the prospect to provide descriptive responses as opposed to yes or no answers. As examples:

- ► How are you approaching Pain No. 1?

- ► What has your experience been pursuing Opportunity No. 2?

- ► Could you share your thoughts on capturing Opportunity No. 3? What's worked and what hasn't?

- ► What happens when Problem No. 4 raises its ugly head? And if the problem is not addressed, what's the impact?

- ► Tell me about your current initiative to achieve Result No. 5.

This is also the time to explore issues the prospect responded to when you delivered your power statement. Circle back and ask why that particular issue piqued the customer's interest. Asking why is usually a good idea as long as you don't do it so frequently that you begin sounding like a three-year-old. Too often we begin answering a prospect's question assuming we know why they asked it. But the simplest way not to head down an unhelpful and unproductive path is to stop, pause, and say, "That's a good question. Why'd you ask that?"

Here's a critical piece of coaching as you progress through these more specific opportunity-seeking questions: Listen to the answers! It's very common to see salespeople so focused on getting all their questions asked that they lose focus on the prospect. Listen intently. Look interested. Take notes. When the prospect's answer doesn't make sense to you, ask for clarification or an example. And most important, when you hit on a topic where it's clear an issue exists, dig deeper. Don't just move on to your next question. Ask follow-up questions. Remember, we're in search of the customer's pains, problems, needs, and desires. If you discover some of these issues, camp out for a while. Go beyond the surface to understand more about those issues. The more you can learn here, the more relevant your questions and persuasively you can address the issues when you begin "selling" in the next phase of the call.

But as mentioned previously, resist the temptation to launch into sales-mode. When you find a scab, pick at it. Keep probing. And when it starts to bleed a little, pick harder. Ask your prospects how they've attempted to conquer the issue and why that hasn't worked. Pour a little salt in the open wound. Find out the consequences of not solving the issue or achieving the desired result. Everything learned at this stage is useful later, especially when the time comes to propose a solution.

Sales Process Questions

This fourth category of questions is designed to help us gather information we need to successfully advance the opportunity through the sales process. Using our aviation analogy again, these questions secure data about air traffic and weather that assist in planning our flight so that we can arrive safely at the desired destination.

Salespeople get excited when discovering a prospect has the very issues they can solve. This excitement causes the salesperson to speed the sales process toward the proposal stage. While responding with a sense of urgency appears to be a good thing, it can also create problems. The fast-moving salesperson forgets to gather important information, which inevitably will stall the sale later in the process.

Think back to your last few deals where the prospect went dark (i.e., stopped responding). Everything seemed great at first. There was interest and need. You connected with the prospect on a personal level, or so you thought. The feedback was positive and you continued edging up the likelihood of closing the deal. But then suddenly and without warning, the prospect went dark. Nothing. No more return calls or replies to e-mails. Crickets.

More often than not, deals go dark when you're blindsided by some factor you didn't discover earlier in the process. Maybe your contact, the person you've been meeting with, truly didn't have authority to buy. Or was there no money to fund a solution. Possibly our definition of "soon" didn't align with your prospect's. Whatever the case, it hurts when your contact stops responding, especially when you already booked the revenue (and spent the commission) in your mind.

It's unlikely you can learn everything you need to during the initial sales call, but it certainly helps to go into that meeting with a clear handle on the factors you want to discover, namely:

- ► Decision authority and decision influencers
- ► Timelines
- ► Available dollars or budget
- ► Willingness to make a change

- Stage in the buying process

- Decision criteria (how the decision will be made, not who makes it)

- Alternative options

- Competition

Great salespeople tackle all of these issues before presenting a proposal. You must fully understand the prospect's situation to give yourself the best shot at winning the business. You don't get paid for working hard and cranking out proposals. You earn your keep closing deals and booking revenue! While it seems counterintuitive, sometimes the best way to speed up closing a deal is to slow down the sales process to gain the necessary information.

I worked with a highly talented, high-level salesperson who was a subject matter expert in her area. In fact, this woman was more of an expert and consultant than a salesperson. We'd go on sales calls and prospects would fall in love with her and what she could do for them. It was common for the prospect to ask for a full-blown proposal for an annual program at the conclusion of a first meeting. Flattered and excited about the opportunity, the salesperson usually would happily comply. The problem, however, was that these proposals were complex and could take up to fifteen hours to prepare. After losing a deal we thought was in the bag and seeing another go dark, we began examining her sales process. It turned out that we were not asking enough questions about decision influencers and the decision process.

You put yourself in a much stronger position to win once you've gathered critical data that helps not only position your proposal, but also work all the variables influencing the decision. It serves your best interests to get comfortable asking these types of questions:

- Along with yourself, who else really cares about this issue? (That is by far the best way to ask about other influencers and your contact's decision-making authority without it coming off as an insult. I did not craft the wording, but have heard it used perfectly by several experts. I am not sure where it originated, but can attest that it is a very useful question to ask.)

► Where are you in the process of evaluating options?

► Where will the money come from to fund this initiative?

► This is a significant decision. How committed are you to making a change? What is the likelihood that you will leave your current supplier (or solution) or change direction?

► Tell me the criteria you'll use to make your decision. How will you decide?

► What other alternatives are on the table?

Deals go dark when you get lazy and shoot from the dark. Practice asking these types of questions at every prospect meeting. You'll become more confident and more skilled at securing the information necessary to successfully move the deal forward.

Sell

Now it's your turn. Finally! Let it fly. Based on what you learned thus far, *sell, sell, sell.*

The patience and discipline you've displayed to this point earned you the right to take center stage. Your prospect is primed to hear how you can help him and his business. You built rapport and credibility, demonstrated professionalism, served an exquisite appetizer that created hunger for more, and gathered copious amounts of information about your prospect. Take full advantage of the solid platform you constructed and launch your strongest sales missiles.

This is the stage of the call when you finally get to act like a salesperson. And because this sales call was structured and conducted so beautifully, you have the ability to weave what's important to the prospect into your sales pitch. Say it aloud with me: DISCOVERY PRE-CEDES PRESENTATION.

Grab your literature. Review fancy charts and graphs. Wax eloquently about your samples. Share stories of how you've helped other clients achieve remarkable results. Describe possible solutions. Flip through a few screens on your iPad, showing off your latest and greatest whiz-bang offering. Provide customer testimonials.

Take full advantage of what you've learned to tailor your message for this particular prospect. Show off your sales skills by showing the buyer that you actually listened. Skip over areas that are not relevant and spend extra time dwelling on key points that will resonate with the buyer's issues. You've identified the prospective buyer's needs, issues, and opportunities; now tie them in directly with your offerings, using the buyer's own words to drive home your points.

Determine Fit and Seek Out Objections

By the time you wrap up the previous phase, where you demonstrated your selling skills, you have a pretty good idea if there's a potential fit with this account. If I'm relatively confident that the prospect is tracking with me, and sense that I can bring value and an appropriate solution, then I start to smile because an opportunity is materializing before my eyes.

I smile, begin gently nodding my head, and say, "Based on our conversation and what we've shared with each other, it looks like we might be a fit to help you." Then I pause to let the thought and moment sink in. If the prospect doesn't respond after a few seconds, I follow with, "What do you think?"

This is a pivotal moment. We need to hear what's on the other person's mind. Were we just imagining and hoping that we connected the dots, or will the prospect affirm that for us? It's imperative that the prospect speak up. Don't feel the need to fill the silence or resort to reselling your main points. Exercise self-control. Ask again what the prospect thinks, and pay attention to the tone and content of the response. If the person is uncomfortable providing too much positive feedback, it may be a sign that you need to ask a few more sales process questions. Are there others in the organization that deserve to hear your sales story? Do you need to repeat this initial meeting? Are there any cultural issues, politics, or competing initiatives possibly making it difficult for your prospect to get excited about what you have to offer?

We're looking for two distinct takeaways from this phase of the call. First, we're seeking confirmation that we indeed have a potential solution for this prospect. Plain and simple: Do we have a fit? Can we help this prospect? Does the prospect think there's potential for us to help his business?

Second, we need to flesh out potential obstacles and objections. I know that seems counterintuitive. Many people in sales want to run and hide from objections. That's silly. The best time to learn about concerns the prospect may have about going forward is right now! If the prospect conveys any reticence or sends a signal that something is just not right, ask about it. Go back to probing. Discovering potential obstacles while sitting face-to-face is the best thing that can happen. It presents an opportunity for you, if possible, to address them on the spot. And it helps you strategize how to work around and overcome those obstacles as the opportunity progresses. If you can tell in your gut that something is amiss, but your contact won't say it, ask directly. Say: "I get the feeling you have concerns or see obstacles about going forward. Tell me what you're thinking. I'd rather hear your concerns now than pretend they don't exist."

Define and Schedule the Next Step

I always enjoy listening to salespeople recap sales calls. There's always something to learn and usually something that makes you laugh. Salespeople like to brag about the great job they did conducting the call. Sometimes the stories take on a life of their own, kind of like fishing stories. Each time the story of the incredible sales call is retold, it becomes more dramatic. The fish gets bigger and the salesperson looks more and more heroic.

There's one question I make every salesperson answer following each call: What's the next step? And more often than you'd think, that next step hasn't been defined. I don't care how great you feel about your meeting with the dream prospect. If you left without defining, agreeing to, and scheduling the next step, then you failed. They loved you and told you so, but you forgot to define the next step for both sides? Fail. You gave the greatest presentation of your life and received a standing ovation, but you left without agreement on the next step? Also a failure. Point taken?

The final stage of a winning sales call is the simplest stage of all. Define what comes next. Once you've discussed whether you may be a fit for the prospect and worked to unearth potential objections, the conclusion of the meeting is easy.

One question—"What do you suggest as an appropriate next step?"—is all it takes to bridge toward agreement on what comes next. It also provides an opportunity for the prospect to direct you and to remain in control. Asking for the other person's thoughts relieves the pressure that traditional closing techniques create. We've spent the previous hour (or however long) conducting a professional, no-pressure, two-way sales conversation. There's no reason to switch gears now and a pull a power-move on the prospect. Let's not destroy the credibility and comfort we've worked so hard to build.

Listen and process the prospect's response. My favorite thing to do at this point is to offer next steps for each of us. I'll say, "Based on what you're saying, how about if I do EFG, and you pull together JKL?" In other words, "Let me do this and you do that." Mutual commitment is a good thing.

However, suggesting the next step only earns you partial credit. You've got to schedule that step. Today, that's easier than ever. Grab your smartphone or open your calendar. There's a high likelihood the prospect will follow your lead. Pick the date that both parties can agree to accomplish an agreed-upon task and confirm what happens next. Repeat it. Book it. Shake on it.

One final thought about ending the call appropriately: Don't fall all over yourself thanking the person for their time. Sure, be thankful; be respectful. But act like you've been here before. You should be accustomed to conducting meetings that end with a positive outcome for both sides. Keep in mind that you've delivered much value to the prospect. You provided ideas; you painted a picture of a successful outcome. So while it's fine to thank the person for investing the time to visit with you, don't bow down in the process. Remember, your prospect is the one with the pain, problem, or desired result. You have the potential solution. If you've done your job by correctly structuring and conducting the sales call, your prospects should be just as appreciative of you as you are of them.

Questions for Reflection

► Have you been conducting sales calls with a logical progression—a beginning, a middle, and an end?

► If you have attempted to share you agenda and lay out your plan for sales calls in the past, how has that approach been received?

► Looking back on your past several sales calls, who was flying the airplane from the pilot's seat—you or the customer?

► Do you think delivering your power statement relatively early in the call earns you enough credibility to ask meaningful, probing questions?

► Have you experimented with different ways to conclude calls by determining if there is a fit, fleshing out objections, and defining next steps?

CHAPTER 12

Preventing the Buyer's Reflex Resistance to Salespeople

There's been a recurring subtheme running like an undercurrent through the previous chapters on the sales story, proactive telephone calls, and sales calls. Just in case I have been a bit subtle (not something I'm often accused of), allow me to pause here to hammer the point home.

Buyers resist salespeople. Everyone does it, even those of us selling for a living. Buyers, especially prospects, have an automatic, almost instinctive, negative reflex reaction to salespeople. You know exactly what I'm referring to because you respond the same way. Think back to your last trip to a furniture store. What thoughts immediately went through your head as the eager, clipboard-carrying salesman approached? Or how about when you received that unexpected call and the telemarketer launched into her script without pause immediately after mispronouncing your name? *"Mr. Winberg, this is Amanda from Mosquitos Have Rights of Missouri. We would like to thank you for helping us out in the past, and this year you can make an enormous impact...."* Shoot me now.

Some of you are thinking, "Come on, that's a retail salesperson or telemarketer. Of course we recoil reflexively when they intrude. But buyers don't respond the same way to me or other business-to-business sales reps, do they?" Yes, they do, and so do you. Remember that last sales guy, the one you granted an appointment and then invited your team to sit in on his presentation? That same guy who blabbered nonstop about irrelevant industry data points and subjected you to a forty-minute demo without asking one meaningful question about your business? Did you and your teammates not immediately begin resisting his message as soon as you realized it was a mistake to invite him in? Of course you did. Everyone puts up some sort of defense shield because salespeople repeatedly give us plenty of cause to do so.

It's Not Your Fault, but It Is Your Problem

This automatic reflex resistance to salespeople is not your fault. You didn't do anything to cause it. You inherited the situation. The waters were poisoned way before you got here. Other morons, whether from retail sales, telesales, or business-to-business sales (as described in the previous examples), messed the whole thing up for us. Unfortunately, we're left to contend with the consequences.

Think for a minute how your friends outside of sales (or even coworkers who are anti-sales) would describe a salesperson. Here are the not-so-flattering words I hear people consistently use when talking collectively about those of us in sales:

- ► Self-absorbed
- ► Manipulative
- ► Verbose
- ► Unreliable
- ► High ego
- ► Pest

- Time waster

- Disconnected from my reality

- Poor listener

Friends, this is what we are up against. Not pretty. We may not have caused it, but it is our problem. And we certainly must deal with it if we're going to succeed.

When was the last time you took a long look and listened to how you are coming across to prospective customers? Have you invested the energy to evaluate each aspect of your sales approach in light of how your actions and words are perceived by the buyer?

My eyes were opened to the importance of that question while working with a client's sales team last year. This great little company had a handful of sales reps; they competed in a tough arena and the business was doing remarkably well compared to its peers. But their success was due to an effective marketing engine that was generating an abundance of leads for this relatively unpolished sales team. A large portion of the reps' job was to sift through the leads and determine which had potential to be converted into "opportunities" they could work. There was consensus among senior management that the sales reps were fumbling the leads and converting an embarrassingly low percentage into deals.

Management's assessment was correct, to say the least. I worked closely with a few of the less seasoned reps, listening to them on outbound calls and leaving voice mail messages. What I heard was disturbing. The reps had zero awareness of how they were coming across to the people they were calling. They cranked through lead after lead at breakneck speed. Every word out of their mouths was self-focused. There was no attempt to connect, relate, or understand. The motivation for calling was transparently selfish and anyone on the other end could smell it.

After an hour biting my tongue, I switched from nice guy observer to coach. I forced this one rookie to stop before each call to articulate his objective and review what he knew about the lead. But as hard as I tried to help him focus on the prospect, he was unable or unwilling to alter his approach. I was embarrassed even listening to him delivering his canned message on the phone. In frustration, I told the young man that he sounded like a cheesy pitchman only interested in accomplishing his own objective for the calls. So, after pushing him to consider how the prospect might perceive his sales tactics, this rookie gave me a treat. He stubbornly responded that he *liked* sounding like a salesperson. In fact, it was his way of qualifying the lead! He reasoned everyone understood that if you're going to buy, you'll need to deal with a salesperson. So be it if he turned off the prospect. That only meant they weren't interested in buying. Needless to say, this young man failed. We set him free to succeed elsewhere, and my hope is that there's now one less uncoachable moron out there giving sales professionals a bad name.

Shaping How the Customer Perceives You

That experience, combined with what I was observing with other clients, had a profound impact on my sales coaching. I concluded that my concern with how buyers perceived salespeople could no longer remain an undercurrent in my coaching. Rather, this topic was worthy of top billing and earned a position front and center.

Buyer's resistance to salespeople is so strong and so prevalent that it requires us to have a second objective for every aspect of our sales attack. Right alongside our primary objective of what we'd we like to accomplish, it is imperative to ask additional questions to ensure we're not thwarting our own sales effort and encouraging the customer to resist us:

- ► How will the prospect or customer feel about you and your company following this interaction?
- ► What message are you sending about the experience the customer will have working with you?

► How can you inform the customer that you understand this interaction is not about you?

► What can be communicated to demonstrate that you are worthy of the prospect's time and are driven to bring maximum value to your potential customer?

We must ask these questions with an eye toward how the potential customer will perceive us. This is particularly true in today's difficult selling environment where the lame approach of so many desperate salespeople only heightens a buyer's sensitivity.

Preventing and Minimizing the Buyer's Resistance

Since we agree that this automatic resistance buyers have toward salespeople is real, it's foolish and naive to pretend it doesn't exist. As professionals, we should expect it and prepare for it. That's why I am adamant that we examine every aspect of our proactive new business pursuit through the filter of the buyer's defense shield. Let's start with an examination of the things we believe about ourselves as salespeople, how we sound, what we say, and our feelings toward our prospects.

Our Beliefs

What we believe about our job and our role as salespeople has a tremendous effect on how buyers see us. If deep down we truly believe that potential customers will be better off working with us, and we have their best interests at heart, buyers will perceive and reward our genuine intentions. We know the opposite is true as well. Buyers detect insincerity as quickly as they can smell cheap cologne. And nothing causes them to raise the defense shield faster than a bad-smelling, phony salesperson.

Representing ourselves as problem solvers who exist to bring value sets us apart from the throng of other salespeople vying for the customer's attention. It also helps when we initiate contact with new potential customers because our motives are right. We want to call on our prospects because we truly believe we can make their job, their life, and their business better. Wise buyers are much slower to resist a salesperson whose clear motivation is to help them succeed.

Our Sound

Sometimes you can detect a salesperson just by listening to the tone and cadence of the individual's voice. This type of salesperson can cause a prospect to react like an annoyed skunk raising its tail. That's why it is surprising that so many salespeople actually try to sound like a salesperson, and like each other. How silly. These mimicking reps accomplish the opposite of what they intend. Instead, they clue the buyer to deploy his defenses, knowing that sales bombs are about to rain down.

As I admonished earlier in the chapter on proactive telephone calls, lose the sales voice. The moment a buyer hears that prototypical sales tone, the yellow caution flag comes out. Most salespeople are unaware they even do this, and yet it destroys their sales approach. Practice speaking in a normal, friendly, casual, confident voice. If you can master a natural demeanor, then there's hope your prospects will actually listen rather than shut their ears at the first sound of the sales voice.

Our View of the Prospect

A client once asked me to study members of his sales organization to discover the main differences between the top and bottom performers. It was a fascinating and energizing experience because it was so different from my typical engagement. The findings were not what I expected going into the assignment. There were indeed subtle differences between those who were struggling and those producing three times the average. These subtleties had a huge impact on how the various reps viewed and approached their leads.

The reps that were struggling maintained two defeatist and destructive assumptions about their leads. The underperforming reps did not enter a dialogue with the leads believing they were serious prospects. They used descriptions like "tire-kickers" and "window-shoppers" when sharing their frustrations about lack of conversions. The second defeatest belief I uncovered revolved around the assumed motive of the buyer. This group of reps was convinced that the leads were simply price shoppers looking to get the cheapest deal possible. It's not hard to predict how these reps came across to their leads, and the results proved it. If you were the buyer, how would you respond to a salesperson who telegraphed his perceptions that you were not a serious prospective customer and your only interest was getting a low-ball price?

In contrast, the top performers at this company had a different view of their leads. They entered the initial conversation with the new lead assuming that it was a legitimate opportunity to make a sale. Leads weren't simply price shopping; they were likely reaching out because they were stuck and looking for help with their situation. Imagine, for a moment, how differently these top reps came across to the leads compared to those who were struggling.

Our Feelings Toward the Prospect

Another difference between high-performing and underachieving sales reps is their own feelings toward the prospect heading into the initial conversation. The successful reps were not only optimistic about their chances of winning the business, they also had warm, positive emotions about the potential customer. One rep went as far as saying, "I love these leads."

Not surprisingly, the reps who were struggling had quite a different set of feelings. Frustrated from their lack of success, the reps in this group often harbored anger toward prospects, even before speaking with them. It was almost as if they were prejudging the leads and projecting their anger and frustration onto innocent potential customers they had yet to engage. It's hard to blame a buyer for resisting the approach of an angry salesperson.

It's safe to say that most salespeople are not great poker players, because we tend not to hide our emotions very well. In all likelihood, we telegraph the emotions we have toward prospects, allowing them to sense our feelings. And when that view is not a positive one, it follows that our prospects would resist our approach to sell to them.

Our Words

Here's one more reminder that buyers couldn't care less about how smart we are or how wonderful we think our company is. Understandably, they are only concerned with what's in it for them. From the first few sentences emanating from our lips, the buyer is determining if we "get it." The conversation is supposed to be about them, not about us. Buyers screen every word we say through this filter. The moment they discern that your focus is on yourself and what you sell, the resistance goes up and you're lumped in the pile with every other self-focused salesperson they try to avoid.

The absolute best way to slow or prevent the buyer's typical reflex resistance is to lead with client issues whenever we communicate. As reviewed in Chapter 8, the power in our sales story comes from that first section of the power statement where we share the reasons that customers turn to us. Buyer will not resist sales messaging that begins with items and issues that are top of mind for them. We must become comfortable and conversant speaking about the pains we remove, problems we solve, and results we achieve for customers. Connecting with prospects in that manner causes them to replace their mental "no soliciting" sign with a bright neon welcome sign.

Buyers have a reflexive resistance to salespeople. We may not have caused that condition, but we are certainly selling against that reality every day. It is up to us to do everything possible to minimize a buyer's indifference or negative predisposition to a sales approach. We can slow or even prevent that resistance by viewing ourselves and the prospect differently, and consciously working to choose words that would cause the buyer to welcome instead of resist us.

Questions for Reflection

► What self-defeating beliefs about yourself and your role as a salesperson are detracting from the way you come across to buyers?

► When you sell, how aware are you that the behavior of other salespeople has potentially damaged how buyers perceive you?

► What can you do to sound different from every other salesperson targeting the very same buyers you are?

► What is your view of your prospects before contacting them? Is that view hurting or helping how you approach buyers?

CHAPTER 13

I Thought I Was Supposed to Make a Presentation

From my earliest days in sales, I've viewed selling as a dialogical exercise. Sales calls, no matter how big or important, are intended to be a two-way conversation. They might take place in the buyer's office, a meeting room, or possibly even the gigantic boardroom. But there's never any thought of standing. Why would anyone stand to have a conversation with a person who's seated? This is supposed to be a sales call, right? A meeting where a buyer and seller discuss relevant topics to determine if it makes mutual sense to do business (or more business) together.

In the mid to late 1990s, concurrent with the rapid proliferation of Microsoft PowerPoint, I began working with more "sophisticated" companies. A new word was added to my sales lexicon—*presentation*—and more than fifteen years later, I still wince every time it is uttered in my presence.

I have come to hate that word, particularly when it's pronounced by salespeople with a long "e." Preezentation. We all have certain words that cause an immediate visceral reaction. (I'm sure yours are coming to mind right about now.) Cancer is top on my list. I hear that word and rage builds inside me. I purse my lips, shake my head, and am ready to unload the most hateful expletives known to man. I. Hate. Cancer. Rosemary (the herb) causes a similar reaction. If there's a more putrid herb or a quicker way to destroy a perfectly fine dish, I'm unaware of it. Rosemary should be banned, and chefs who use it without bold warning on the menu should be charged with malpractice. Presentation slots nicely right between cancer and rosemary as a word that triggers violent explosions in my brain.

Why I Hate the Word *Presentation*

When I first learned about PowerPoint and was taught the concept of making presentations to prospects and buyers, it was a bit intimidating. The thought of being center stage, before potential customers, messed with my mind and created a pressure I was not accustomed to. I already had experienced tremendous success and had conducted my share of high-stakes sales calls with giant companies. None of those experiences made me nervous, but there was something different, awkward, and I'll dare say, even wrong with the dynamic surrounding presentations.

I eventually became comfortable using PowerPoint as a tool to help communicate. But philosophically, I still could not get my arms around this practice of presenting to prospects, especially early in the sales process. It didn't matter how *en vogue* presentations had become. I was, am, and will remain convinced that the entire concept is flawed.

In the spring of 2000, barely a few weeks into my time at the web-based learning management system company described in Chapter 4, I experienced the most painful, formative, and valuable lesson of my sales career.

Our little firm was aligned with a very large performance improvement company. We had a deal setting up this behemoth organization as a channel partner. It made sense on the surface. They had a comprehensive learning offering and many Fortune 500 companies as clients. This company's crack team of highly compensated senior account managers was spread across the United States, and the hope was that their sales force would open doors and uncover opportunities to sell our learning management system.

We received a call from our partner's learning team. One of their top salespeople, a perennial recipient of president's club status, had scored a presentation and demo for us at one of his major accounts. Everyone at our company was ecstatic and there was lots of talk about how best to conduct the demo. Personally, I was confused about the process and not quite sure why we would be "presenting," since this was an initial meeting with the client. But as the eager and respectful newbie, I played along nicely and kept quiet. For the record, that was the last time in my life I stayed quiet about sales process or a sales opportunity.

Having only been with the company a few weeks, I was in no way prepared to handle this opportunity. It was decided that our vice president, Mark (who also happened to be the friend who recruited me into the company), would lead our portion of the presentation and conduct the demo. He was intimately familiar with the system and also had a better handle on the inner workings of this channel partner. I was simply along for the ride and education. And what an education it turned out to be!

The major account was an electronics company with its U.S. headquarters in New Jersey. Mark and I plunked down more than $1,000 each to fly in and out of Newark for the big meeting. Not a minor expenditure for a company of our size.

Our partner's sales star—I'll call him Frank—picked us up at the airport. It was a rainy dreary day, which was an appropriate backdrop for what was about to take place. On the ride from the airport, Frank shared that the division president accepted his invitation to attend the presentation. Impressive. I was obviously in excellent hands and excited to learn from this sales pro.

Frank assured us that he had it covered. The plan was for him to "tee up the demo" (his exact words) with a brief presentation. He would run through just a few slides highlighting his company's relationship with the account. That would give the committee a glimpse into how entrenched Frank was in other areas of their business and provide plenty of credibility to set up our demo. After covering this introductory material, Frank would introduce our company as a technology partner, and we'd conduct a full-blown demonstration of our "best thing since sliced bread" learning management system.

Are you getting uncomfortable yet as I tell this story? I am, and you should be. A lot could have been done differently up to this point. Even though I was the rookie with the ink still wet on my business cards, I knew better. Instead of speaking up about my discomfort, I took a pass and deferred to the supposed sales star. Heck, it was his account and he was the guy winning annual trips to Aruba as a consistent top performer. I was plenty confident in my guy, Mark. He is as professional as anyone I know, plus I had seen him masterfully show off the benefits of our learning platform. So even if I didn't agree with Frank's approach, I figured Mark could come in from the bullpen to earn the save.

We passed through security and were directed to the corporate boardroom. Not just any conference room, but The Boardroom. The room had more square footage than my house, and the gorgeous table easily sat sixty people. We began to set up, and within a few minutes the members of the committee entered the room. Unfortunately, we were more concerned about the Internet connection than we were about connecting with this team. That should have been a red flag. It certainly was a prophetic sign of what was to come.

We nervously got everything working and began to settle into premeeting small talk. Frank stood at the head of the table. The division president walked in, greeted everyone, and said bluntly, "Good to see you, Frank. I only have thirty minutes, then I need to leave." He sat down in the chair closest to Frank. The train wreck that ensued is burned in my memory bank as vividly as any moment in my entire career. That's how painful and life changing the lesson was. And it is why, to this day, I harbor such deep hatred toward the word *presentation*.

Frank went. And went. And went. Not a single question made its way out of his mouth—slide after self-focused slide. It was a sight to behold. It was a surreal, almost unbelievable experience. In fact, if you saw a cartoon strip or *Saturday Night Live* parody of his presentation, you'd conclude it had to be fictional. No one would actually do what Frank did that day.

First came multiple slides showing pictures of buildings on his company's large campus. Yes, this actually happened. In the most impressive boardroom I have ever visited, in front of the division president of one of the most well respected companies in the world and a committee charged with selecting the very solution we sold, Frank put up not one, not two, but three slides with pictures of buildings to begin his presentation.

I looked over at Mark with big eyes. He was frozen in a catatonic state, and I wasn't sure he would survive the meeting. I kept thinking, surely Frank is going to ask something of the committee. Something simple, something easy like, "Francine, Steven, Joyce, Joe, could you tell us why you were selected to lead the search for a learning management system?" Or maybe something even easier, such as, "What were you hoping to get from us today?" Would it have been too much to ask, "What business issues are driving this initiative?" Nothing. Nada. No questions. He was clearly too busy *teeing up* our demo.

Following the pictures of the lovely corporate campus came two slides with the logos of big-name clients that Frank's company served. Really. Five slides in and I am having childhood flashbacks to *The Gong Show*. Only Frank is just getting warmed up, and there's no gong in sight.

Slides six, seven and eight are beautiful flowcharts of his company's performance improvement process. Frank waxes on eloquently about the company expertise in several areas. At this point, the committee is sitting silently, Mark is red-faced, and I'm freaking out thinking about how my little company flushed two grand of airfare down the toilet so that we could watch this joker in his black blazer worn over a golf shirt babble endlessly about his employer's majestic buildings, clients, and processes.

Twenty-two minutes into Frank's presentation, the division president is visibly frustrated. He interrupts Frank by saying, "I'd like to see the demo, please." Frank speeds through a few more slides and turns it over to Mark. Great tee up, eh? Let's just say that's not exactly what we had in mind.

Sensing it was too far gone to redirect the meeting or begin engaging the committee members, Mark respectfully responded to the president's request and began the demo. He executed a crisp, abbreviated demonstration of the platform and some of our flashiest custom-designed content. Honestly, he did a fantastic job under the circumstances. Miraculously, he didn't come off as angry and flustered, and he made the best of an impossible situation. After about ten minutes, the president thanked us for coming and excused himself. Thud.

Mark took another ten minutes to finish showing off the system and then the room fell silent. Eerily silent. Sales star Frank sat quietly. The members of the committee all looked over at me, maybe because I had not said a word up to this point. Mark nodded at me. I glared at Frank like he was an enemy of the state. I should have said aloud what I was thinking to myself: "This is the guy who wins the president's club trip every year?"

I took a deep breath and thanked the committee for investing the time to visit with us. Then I cringed, already anticipating the answer to the question I was about to ask: "Was what we shared today on target with what you are looking for from a web-based learning management system?" They answered no. They didn't think it was what they were looking for. The committee thanked us and left us the room.

On the way back to the airport Frank kept talking, but I stopped listening after he declared how rude the committee was to us. His perspective was as laughable as his presentation.

As I said, this was the most painful and valuable experience of my sales career. And I'm so thankful it occurred. The next day I wrote an entire document recapping what took place on that expensive and frightful day in New Jersey. I promised myself and anyone who would listen that it would never happen to me again. Never.

Along with cementing my hatred of the word *presentation,* that day provided several meaningful lessons that I carry with me to this day:

▶ No matter how senior or entrenched my selling partners, managers, or coworkers, I will never again cede control of the selling process to someone else. I am responsible for executing a solid sales process, regardless of who owns the account relationship.

▶ When something doesn't feel right that's because it's not right. Don't go along for the ride, even in the name of education or training. Speak up. Ask hard questions. I have a good sales gut and need to trust it.

▶ By sales law, a first meeting cannot be a presentation. Ever.

▶ Even when asked to do a presentation, turn it into a dialogue by asking questions throughout the meeting, but especially in the beginning.

In all fairness, I must share one more thing about that story before moving on. Miraculously, somehow, some way, we ended up winning that deal. It took months longer than it needed to. But good ole Frank and the team found a way to get the train back on the tracks, which is a testament to the power of a deep client relationship combined with having a great solution. After dishing out all that abuse to Frank, I must give credit where credit is due. In no way does that excuse the total train wreck created by his complete bungling of that meeting. Every detail I shared is true. It really was that bad. And that horrendous experience served as a catalyst that put me on the path to my current life as a sales coach and consultant.

Redeeming the PowerPoint Presentation

While I have made it abundantly clear how I feel about the word, the reality is that a killer presentation, made at the right time and structured the right way, can be one of our most powerful sales weapons. And to ensure that the presentation gun is aimed at the prospect, not pointed so that you shoot your own sales effort in the foot, it's essential that the focus of the presentation be squarely on the customer.

We have all suffered through terrible PowerPoint presentations on both sides of the table. We've been puked on by salespeople, and we've been guilty of puking on others. But let's be clear: PowerPoint in and of itself is not evil. It's what we do with PowerPoint that's a sin. PowerPoint enables our tendency to create presentations that become monologues, painfully long monologues all about our company, our processes, our people, and our perfect solution.

I often tell people, *"No one cares how smart you are or how great you think your company is."* In fact, that favorite expression of mine came out of that horrific meeting with Frank and the electronics company. I say it all the time to remind everyone within earshot that our presentations need not be about ourselves and our companies. The hard truth is that unless you're selling for NASA or another rocket-science organization, do yourself a favor and lose the slides with the pretty pictures of your buildings. Trust me, they are not helping you advance the sale.

I propose a simple four-slide recipe that ensures the early focus of your presentation is where it belongs:

Slide 1: Title Slide

Slide 2: Suggested Agenda

Slide 3: Companies Turn to (Insert Your Company Name) When . . . (Here you'll want to grab three to five relevant bullets from the "client issues" section of your power statement.)

Slide 4: Our Understanding of Your Situation . . .(List several items you have learned from discovery work up to this point.)

Slide 4 is absolutely critical because this is where we transition from the generic, broad statements in slide 3 to the prospect-specific issues we have uncovered *prior to* making the presentation. It's our opportunity to show off the thorough discovery work we have completed thus far. We also benefit from the relationships we've built with various players and their constituencies in the prospect's organization. The very fact that we can list these issues bears witness to the investment we've made to understand their business.

Once you have reviewed the data on slide 4, I want to ask you to do something dangerous and unthinkable for many salespeople: *Convert this presentation from a monologue into a dialogue.*

Tell the audience that you think it would be beneficial to stop at this slide for a while. Ask your audience for input. Where did you nail it right on the head? What issues did you misunderstand or not properly grasp? Even better, ask the most senior person in the room to rank or prioritize the items on that slide. Make every effort to confirm the assumptions you're sharing. If time allows and the prospect seems willing, dig deeper with specific probing questions. See if you can reopen a wound or pour salt in one that's bleeding, as we discussed in Chapter 11. That is, ask about the consequences resulting from the issues they face, and what might happen if they're not properly addressed. Not only are we scoring sales points demonstrating our expertise by asking these questions, but we are again gleaning perspectives on how to best tailor the balance of our presentation. The more we can learn, even right here in the midst of a supposed "presentation," the better we are able to customize our pitch.

Discovery Must Precede Presentation, so Insist on a Meeting

Every day, salespeople fail because they mistake presenting for selling. Presenting is not selling; it's only a part of the sales process. Many salespeople are lazy and don't want to put the hard work into researching accounts, developing relationships, and performing the necessary heavy lifting and discovery work before making a presentation. Others are not lazy, but simply prefer presenting because they enjoy the lime-light and hearing the sound of their own voice.

The hard truth is that if we are not in a position to create slide 4 because we don't have the necessary information, then we should not be making a presentation—even if asked to by the customer. Let me repeat that: If you have not completed enough discovery work to be able to list a handful of bullets describing the prospect's current situation, then you have absolutely no business conducting a presentation. The fact that the prospect requested or even insisted you make a presentation doesn't make it right or smart for you to comply. Remember, presenting is not a synonym for selling. The goal is to win business, not simply to follow the directions of a prospect.

So what can you do? Insist on a meeting before the requested presentation. Assert yourself. Let your potential customers know that you have a process for delivering maximum value, and that process entails several critical steps before presenting to them. Explain that if they want your best, they must be willing to help provide what's needed for you to create the optimum solution and presentation specifically for them.

Will that be difficult in some situations? Absolutely. What I am proposing is a foreign concept to many prospects and salespeople alike. It's easier just to comply and go along with the way business is typically conducted. Why rock the boat when the path of least resistance is to simply say yes, show up, and present the standard "capabilities overview" or dog and pony show. You know, kind of how I kept my mouth shut and let Frank completely derail that meeting with the electronics company. I certainly could have spoken up to challenge the process. But why suggest a smarter and more effective way of doing something if the traditional way is easier? The choice is yours. You can define your sales process to give yourself the best shot at differentiating your company and your presentation. Or you can default to the buyer's process and do what you're told.

When the Prospect Will Not Meet with You before the Presentation

Some of you are reading this and philosophically agreeing with me. However, you're also thinking that I'm out of touch or don't fully understand your particular situation. You would very much like to spend time with prospects before delivering presentations, but in your world, that is not reality.

For example, you are a small company calling on massive corporations that have layers of procurement personnel and pages of purchasing protocol. Standard fare in your industry is responding to requests for proposals within stringent guidelines. In many cases, the rules of engagement laid out by the prospect prohibit you from even speaking with key businesspeople at the company issuing the RFP.

It's stupid and perplexing that a company actively prevents its potential business partners from developing relationships, performing important discovery work, and crafting a customized presentation and proposal. These companies have made the intentional decision that they don't want your best work; they're not interested in your creative ability to understand their situation; they're fine with receiving a generic response. In effect, these companies are choosing a lesser solution for the sake of controlling the selling and buying process. It's maddening. And all this is done in the name of fairness, under the banner of creating a level playing field, or in deference to some purchasing agents who took a few courses to become certified procurement analysts. It's wrong. It's stupid. But it's the new reality many in sales must face today.

Yes, I concede there are going to be times when we are absolutely prevented from meeting with prospects and denied the opportunity to understand their situation before having to present to them. There are also some unique industry norms where making pitches and presentations are par for the course.

I coach a local, fast-growing, boutique advertising agency. The founder and CEO had thirty years of experience on the client side before she launched this agency four years ago. She and her team brought me in to help design a business development role. While they have continued to grow at a rapid clip from word of mouth, they've not been very successful proactively acquiring new accounts.

The CEO informed me about an upcoming pitch the agency would be making to a potential client. In the agency world, *pitch* is the equivalent to my favorite word, *presentation*. I knew where the conversation would end up, but I couldn't resist my chance to upset the apple cart to make a point.

I asked a few questions about the prospect and why this company had invited my client in. No one was sure of the answer. Then I asked how they would know what to pitch if they were unsure about the prospect's situation. After some hemming and hawing about it "just being the way things are done" when companies are looking for new agencies, my client finally admitted the truth. They were going in blind to do a capabilities overview and a dog and pony show (their exact words). I had to smile. *Wow.* A company we have never spoken with and don't know anything about asked us to come in and make a pitch to be its new agency. And without pushing back at all, we just said yes and plan to charge ahead blindly? Hmmm.

My client got the point, and we ended up having an enlightening conversation about how to better handle these types of opportunities. My bottom-line recommendation was a bold alternative to the typical "spray and pray" pitch that was the norm. The agency's executive team members would still show up for the pitch, but now they'd treat the hour as if they were conducting a slightly abbreviated version of the sales call structure (outlined in Chapter 11). In other words, if the prospective customer cannot or will not meet with us before the scheduled time for the presentation, then we should convert the first portion of the presentation into the discovery session we never got to conduct.

The following example could apply to the RFP response, to the agency pitch, and even to the situation I once encountered with Frank and the electronics company. For the sake of continuity, I'll stick with the agency story and share my recommendation about how to smoothly and slyly avoid presenting before understanding more about the prospect.

The salesperson who will be leading the "pitch" meeting should take charge after introductions and rapport building. In a very calm and confident manner, as if she handles these discussions every day without resistance, the salesperson should lay out the agenda for the hour, as follows:

We're thrilled to be considered as a potential new agency and business partner for your company, and we look forward to discovering if we are a good fit for each other. Here's how we like to work.

We brought all kinds of goodies with us ... case studies, storyboards, comps, a few examples from our portfolio. We have a few slides outlining our philosophy and approach to helping clients grow business, and we have about a dozen client websites that we can pull up. Honestly, we probably have four hours of content we could share. So, in order for us to present the most relevant and valuable information to you, we'd like to take the first fifteen minutes to get a handle on why you invited us in and what you're facing in your business today—including threats, opportunities, shifts in the marketplace. And if you're willing, we wouldn't mind hearing about your experience with the current or previous agency. We understand if you may not want to "go there," but sometimes clients like to share on that point, so we can incorporate the pieces you like and stay far away from those you don't.

Then, based on what we hear, we will be able to spend the remaining time presenting our best and most appropriate stories, examples, and methodology, and we can skip over areas we don't think would interest you. So, if that's okay, let's do this: I'm going to ask Stephanie, our CEO, to take just three minutes and share the highlights of our agency, why she started the company, and the reasons many of our clients selected us to help grow their business. Then we'll spend some time asking a few questions and hearing from your team so that we can decide, on the fly, what makes the most sense to present. We have found that our prospective clients appreciate this approach. Plus, it provides a little bonus entertainment as you get to watch us create the pitch in real time and argue among ourselves which are the most relevant stories and ideas to share.

To me, that's the difference between presenting and selling. Does it take guts? You bet it does. Will you set yourself apart and leave a memorable impression on the potential client? No doubt about it.

Break the Mold to Set Yourself Apart

For those of you who are highly relational, low-conflict, rule followers, I am sure this idea of partial noncompliance makes you uncomfortable. I understand this approach may stretch you a bit. Sure, it would be easier just to show up and do what everyone else is doing. Pitch away. Easier, yes, but not safer. There's nothing safe about going head-to-head against four competitors who are all using the same strategy and trying hard to differentiate themselves with slight nuances in their presentations. I would argue that it's a more dangerous approach with a lower chance of winning.

We are in sales. Making friends with the rule-writer by complying with every request is not the goal. The objective is to win the business. And our best chance of winning occurs when we understand as much as possible about the prospect's situation before rushing into a presentation. It's even better if we can set ourselves apart and pique the prospect's interest by deploying a smarter sales methodology.

Imagine you are getting ready to hire a professional to completely remodel the kitchen in your thirty-five-year-old home. You did your homework and selected four professionals, all with outstanding reputations. Three came to your house with very similar approaches. They all brought nice binders with pictures of previous jobs, gorgeous brochures from premium cabinet manufacturers, and letters of recommendation from clients in your zip code. Every one of the three was courteous, professional, and apparently highly qualified for the project. Each spent some time measuring and plotting your current kitchen layout on graph paper. For the most part, their pitches were alike, although they all emphasized slightly different aspects of their expertise.

Now imagine that the fourth guy competing for the remodeling job, whom I'll call Jerry (since this is a true story about my kitchen), took a totally different tact. Jerry came in with a big confident smile and asked if it was okay for him to nose around our kitchen. He's opening pantries, asking about the age of our children and whether we may get a dog in the future. Jerry spins the old Lazy Susan and wonders aloud which of those little appliances are used most frequently. Then he points at the oddly placed, boxed soffit on the far wall and declares without shame, "That's weird. I wonder what's in there." He runs out to his truck and comes back with a skinny little saw, a mirror, and a flashlight. Just before cutting into it without permission, Jerry asks how likely we are to do this project in the near future. The moment we assure him that we are absolutely going to remodel this old kitchen, he begins cutting a hole big enough to insert his mirror and flashlight.

Jerry sweeps up the drywall dust from his cutting exercise and sits down next to us at the table. He does not open up a binder or start handing out cabinet brochures. Instead, he looks at my wife and asks, "What is your vision for this room?" Without pausing, Katie points to where she imagines an island with stools. "I see my kids sitting here after school, eating cookies, and telling me about their day." Need I go on? Jerry won our business. Slam dunk. Not even close.

So back to my question: In sales, are you safer following the crowd and the rules, hoping to differentiate yourself with slight variations in your presentation? Or is that actually riskier than breaking out of the mold in an attempt not only to set yourself apart, but also to best connect with your prospect?

Jerry did an extremely nice job on our kitchen, but it was his sales ability that I'll never forget. The second he cut into my wall I made the decision to hire him. It wasn't just that he was so bold. It was that he had to know what was in that soffit in order to craft the solution. What a great visual demonstration of why discovery must precede presentation! The same applies to the question he asked my wife. I'm sure he didn't expect her to reveal her lifelong dream of having the kids at home, eating her cookies while sitting at the island. But the moment she said it, he also knew it was over. (And I bet his price went up a bit, too.)

I like to think about how different that painful day with Frank and the electronics company might have been. What if instead of Frank kicking off the presentation with nine boring, self-focused slides, I had requested that he allow me five minutes to get the meeting off on the right foot? I could have stood at the easel with the giant blank pad and marker, or just sat at the table with a clean sheet of paper. Either would have worked fine. I could have started by thanking Frank and his fine company for introducing us to his important and valued customer. I could have looked at the division president, thanked him for attending, and shared that in order to provide the most value for his half-hour, I needed to use the first five minutes to ensure the next twenty-five would hit the bull's-eye. Then I could have turned to the committee members and asked so easily and innocently...

- ► Why did you invite us in today?

- ► Why were you selected for the committee, and which business issues are you hoping to address with a learning management system?

- ► What does success look like a year after installing the new system? How about three years?

- ► If there was one thing you would like to come away with today, what would that be?

Be leery when you're asked to make a presentation, or when a prospect you were not pursuing requests that you come in and make a pitch. I don't know who decided that selling meant standing at the head of the table and lecturing potential customers, like you're the college professor and they're the students. Presenting is not selling. It is only a part of the selling process. And by sales law, an initial meeting shall never be a presentation. Never.

CHAPTER 14

Planning and Executing the Attack

We have covered a lot of territory, laying the groundwork for a highly successful new business sales attack, and have arrived at the place where the rubber meets the road. There is an endless supply of people in sales who love to talk selling. They've got all kinds of theories. They are masters at philosophizing and pontificating. They would be perfect hosts for the nine-hour Super Bowl Pregame Show: lots of talk and fluff to fill space, analyzing dozens of storylines from every conceivable angle. Have you noticed how many salespeople excel at talking about what they're going to do? And how few actually do what they say? As you read that, I bet certain salespeople are popping into your mind. Big on talk, short on action. It's not an admirable moniker, but it's an all-too-common trait among those making a living, or at least attempting to, in sales.

All the concepts discussed prior to this chapter are meaningless if there's no commitment to action. It's all academic unless we take the field and begin running plays. Working out in the preseason and studying the playbook won't put points on the scoreboard.

We have selected targets and created weapons, so now it is time to start shooting.

No One Defaults to Prospecting Mode

I have consistently observed something intriguing about salespeople: *No one defaults to prospecting. No one.* We don't "happen into" prospecting. New business development is the opposite of driving a car on familiar roads. Isn't it bizarre how we can pull out of our driveway and fifteen minutes later end up where we want without ever giving a conscious thought to controlling the car? Unfortunately, that isn't how it works in sales. I wish it did, but that's not our reality.

There are incredibly few dedicated new business development hunters whose sole responsibility entails opening doors and closing deals. Instead, the overwhelming majority of us in sales roles have a myriad of responsibilities beyond hunting for new business. We have existing account relationships that require attention. There are intra-office relationships with coworkers. There are the sales team meetings, one-on-one meetings with the manager, and interdepartmental meetings. There are questions and interruptions from production or project managers. There are customer service fires raging out of control. And, of course, there are personal distractions: sick kids, a hot stock tip, your favorite professional team making it to the postseason, aging parents, the broken furnace, and your obsession with checking the news and weather every hour.

My point? No one defaults to prospecting. We don't find ourselves with a free half-hour and decide to grab our target list and begin launching weapons. It doesn't happen. In fact, the opposite does. We start out the day with good intentions. There might even be the desire to carve out some proactive time for prospecting. But then life happens. Your biggest customer's order is going to be late and you need to spring into action. Your morning is spent alternating between being master apologizer to the customer and chief beggar with your operations people. Then there's that arduous RFP still sitting on your desk as the deadline for the response inches closer. The CFO e-mails with concerns about your pricing on a major project and also mentions that your chronically late paying customer has gone over ninety days past due again. A very important sales trip is only seven days away and you haven't booked your flight, car, or hotel. You finally remember to get online only to discover that the world's largest convention coincides with your trip and there isn't a car or hotel room anywhere to be found—at least not for what you are allowed to pay.

How familiar is the scenario just described? Some version of that scene seems to be taking place at every company I visit. That is the reality facing salespeople. And you know what suffers, don't you? New Sales. The very same people failing to achieve their new business acquisition numbers are the ones not making proactive selling time a priority.

It doesn't matter whether salespeople are happily distracted from prospecting or they are truly victims of circumstances and their environment. In either case, they are not spending a sufficient amount of time focused on their new business sales attack. And the results prove it.

Time Blocking

It is rare for anyone to argue with my premise. Most people freely admit that their commitment to new business development is not what it should be. Admitting a problem exists is a healthy first step on the road to recovery.

In Chapter 2, I explained how poor use and protection of the calendar is one of the most prevalent reasons salespeople fail at new business development. I don't like talking about time management because it sounds childish and comes across like a never-ending problem. But I love preaching about *time blocking,* because it's one of the simplest and easily implementable concepts. Oh yeah, it also works!

Time blocking is the act of making appointments with yourself for activities that are priorities. It allows us to regain control of our calendars, reorient our schedules, and ensure that blocks of time are dedicated to essential initiatives. The idea is stupidly simple, yet completely foreign to most salespeople.

Since no one prospects by accident and almost no one succeeds doing it in a onesie-twosie fashion, we must carve out significant blocks of time in the calendar for proactive prospecting. And in our crazy business world today, where somehow it became acceptable and permissible for other people to put appointments on our calendars, it is ever more important that we get there first to protect prime selling time. As an aside, it's beyond ridiculous that any joker in your company can see your electronic calendar and schedule a meeting for you. Maybe certain types of people think it's cool when others fill up their calendars for them. I think it's obscene. My time is mine. Don't touch it. Thank you very much.

Decide how much time you should be dedicating to new business development and schedule time blocks at various times throughout the week and month. I can't arbitrarily declare the right amount for you, but from my experience coaching others, I can offer a few suggestions. We tend to be more effective and more confident when we get on a roll. It takes time to settle in and find the groove, so I'd suggest a minimum of ninety minutes per time block. Three hours is probably the limit on the upside, because it's hard to focus for that long and other duties will also come calling. In terms of how often, that depends on your goals. For those doing almost no prospecting now, two time blocks per week, each scheduled for two hours, could produce exponentially better results. For salespeople with significant account acquisition goals, it's conceivable to block out eight or nine of these two-hour new business sessions per week, which still amounts to only about one-third of our working hours.

There are three keys to success for time blocking. The first is to put the time blocks into your calendar. Not just in your mind, but in your calendar. Block the time. The second key is to actually keep the appointment with yourself. Treat this time as sacrosanct. It's as important as any other slot on your calendar. As Jerry Seinfeld said to the rental car agent in one hysterical episode, "You know how to take the reservation, you just don't know how to hold the reservation, and that's really the most important part, the holding. Anybody can just take them!" It's one thing to put the prospecting time blocks on your calendar, but what's the point if you aren't serious about keeping the appointment to do it?

The final key is to remain on task throughout the scheduled time block. Personally, I have found this to be the biggest challenge. Many of us in sales have a hard time focusing. Isn't that part of the reason we ended up in sales in the first place? Well, that characteristic works against us when attempting to lock in on a behavior for a two-hour period. It is imperative to stay in outbound mode. Do not check e-mail. If you must keep your e-mail open because you're using it for prospecting, don't look at your inbox! One e-mail from a friend or an important client who needs something can derail your entire time block. Put your phone on DND. No inbound calls allowed when prospecting. Listen to me: You are not a heart surgeon. No one is going to die on the table because you can't be located for an hour or two. If the building is on fire, someone will come get you. Otherwise, remain laser focused on prospecting. Whatever e-mails and calls you miss in the course of a couple hours can be handled after completing your time block.

Why am I so extreme on this point? Because there are a thousand salespeople failing at new business development for every one salesperson who is failing to serve the needs of existing customers. You likely purchased this book seeking help, ideas, and perspective on how to more effectively prospect and acquire new business. One of the most important takeaways I can provide is that in order to improve new business development results, you must spend more time prospecting. Period.

The Math Works; Work the Math

I don't win many popularity contests with this proclamation. We have all heard it before. Sales is a numbers game. I dislike hearing that as much as the next guy. It isn't complimentary; it doesn't make us feel smart or important. I get that. But it doesn't make the statement any less true: The math works.

Most top-performing salespeople are the most active salespeople. Particularly when it comes to developing new business, the most effective attack is a high-frequency attack. There are lots of tools and toys attempting to help salespeople predict which prospects are best qualified and most ready to buy. And I'm all for new technology, improved data, and as much assistance as possible figuring out which prospects to pursue. But there is one truth from which we cannot escape: The more prospects we meet from our strategically chosen, focused, finite target list, the more opportunities we are likely to uncover. Remember, we are not chasing every Tom, Dick, and Harry walking down the street. The very first step in the New Sales Driver process is selecting targets to pursue for new business. Assuming we did that well, then we know exactly which targets we want to get in front of.

Every business and every salesperson should have a handle on some type of sales math as it relates to the progression of a potential sale through the stages of the process. Over time, when engaged in enough sales activity to produce a relevant sample of data, we should know, on average, how much activity at the beginning of the sales process it takes to produce a closed sale. Let's consider a generic company; here's a list of the stages of its sales process:

1. Prospect targeted.

2. Initial conversation.

3. Meaningful dialogue/first meeting.

4. Prospect needs identified; fit established; mutual agreement to move forward.

5. Second meeting/key data received.

6. Presentation and/or proposal delivered.

7. Deal closed and won!

Again, each business has its own version of something resembling these stages. Working the math comes into play when we can work backward from a closed deal to determine how much new business activity is required to make a sale. For illustration purposes, let's say we win one out of every three proposals we deliver (I understand that every opportunity is different and each deal has its own likelihood of success, but play along with the averages). Three out of four prospects where we have identified needs and believe there's a fit agree to review a formal proposal. Continuing to work backward, history shows that two-thirds of the prospects with whom we conduct initial meetings or have meaningful conversations move to the next step. And finally, our data show that half the prospects we have a first conversation with agree to an initial meeting. For grins, let's say our sales goal this season is to close twelve new deals. Playing out the sales math from the end and working backward, this is what we should expect in terms of activity:

12 closed deals requires 36 proposals delivered (we win one of three).

36 proposals requires 48 opportunities reaching stages 4 and 5, where needs are identified and we believe there is a fit and have a second meeting (three-fourths reaching those stages move to the proposal stage).

48 prospects with needs identified requires 72 initial meetings (two-thirds from first meetings move to the next stage).

72 initial meetings requires 144 initial proactive conversations (half of those turn into initial meetings).

Obviously, the math is different for every business, and it's easy for cynics to poke holes in this example. But the point remains. We need to put a certain amount of new business activity into the top of the sales funnel to generate the amount of closed new business we need coming out the bottom. Sure, we can improve our skills and increase the conversion percentages from stage to stage. The more proficient you become at firing the weapons (discussed from Chapters 7 through 13) the more efficient your sales math becomes. Imagine how the whole math chain would be altered if we could increase the number of proposals we close from only one-third to one-half, or if two-thirds instead of one-half of our initial conversations turned into meaningful dialogues and first meetings.

Understanding your personal sales math provides the backdrop necessary to establish key activity metrics for yourself. It is tremendously helpful to know how much activity you need to generate in order to hit your sales goal. Generally, we cannot control the result, but we certainly can control the volume of activity.

Writing Your Individual Business Plan

One of the best ways to ensure we plan and execute the sales attack, time-block our calendars, and work the math is to write an annual business plan. I'm a huge proponent of salespeople writing an individual business (sales) plan each year. We have all read studies citing that people who write down their goals are many times more successful than those who don't. More than just a mechanism to declare our goals, business plans also serve as a helpful guide to keep us on course. The process of preparing the plan fosters creative, big-picture thinking and also forces salespeople to take ownership of their business (territory, portfolio, etc.).

Individual business plans come in all shapes and sizes, but there are five key components I ask salespeople to include in any plan:

1. *Goals—What You Are Going to Achieve.* It is important to start with the end in mind. The plan should declare personal goals

for the year. Here are some possible categories for which a salesperson would provide specific goals:

► Total revenue dollars

► Gross profit (dollars or percentage)

► Number of new accounts acquired

► Net new business dollars

► Revenue dollars from existing accounts

► Product category, cross-sell, or new product goals

► Major goals for specific named accounts

► Personal income goals (obviously a private objective, but many money-motivated reps are driven to hit certain income targets and find it very helpful to write them down and monitor progress throughout the year)

2. *Strategies—How You Are Going to Do It.* The goals are the "what" and the strategies are the "how." This is the place to spell out how you plan to attack the market and where the business is going to come from. For instance:

► Are there certain existing accounts where you plan on investing extra energy? Some reps provide lists of focus accounts (i.e., largest, most growable) for the year.

► Which geographies, vertical industries, or channels will you pursue? Do you have a focused, finite target prospect list to attach to the plan?

► What major cross-sell opportunities exist within existing accounts?

► How will you approach new accounts? What will you do to get in the door and how will you move opportunities forward?

► What other strategies or tools will you use (e.g., team

selling, events, referral sources, social media connections) to achieve your sales goals?

3. *Actions—Specific Sales Activities You Will Commit To.* List key activity metrics you will measure, monitor, and hold yourself accountable to reach. Examples might include:

   ► Number of hours time-blocked and committed to proactive new business development

   ► Number of outbound calls, number of meaningful conversations, number of face-to-face sales calls

   ► Number of trips to key markets, number of major presentations, number of facility tours or client visits

   ► Number of proposals delivered, dollars proposed

4. *Obstacles—What's in the Way?* Failure is not an option and we don't believe in excuses. I'm of the mindset that if there are obstacles in your way that will prevent you from achieving your goals, you probably know what they are right now. Put them on the table so that they can be addressed, and ask for help or assistance in areas where you need it. Possible obstacles may include:

   ► Product knowledge

   ► Sales support

   ► Lack of technology

   ► Distractions or the company's anti-sales department

   ► Current account management and customer service burdens

   ► Personal health or family issues

5. *Personal Development—How You Plan to Grow This Year.* What are the areas you would like to develop to increase your skills, become more effective, or further your career? Your options may include:

- ► Seminars and conferences to attend

- ► Books and blogs to read

- ► Specific industry training you desire

- ► Expanding your writing skills, social media involvement, or association memberships

- ► Peer coaching or seeking out a mentor

Writing individual business plans is a great exercise. Presenting them to your peers is even better! I like to see sales teams set aside the good part of a day to come together and have each member of the team present her plan to the group. Allot thirty minutes per person—twenty minutes for the presentation and another ten for feedback and Q & A.

So much good happens when plans are shared. It creates instant accountability. Now the entire sales team, along with management, has seen in writing and heard from your mouth what you have committed to do. That is powerful. It's also a great opportunity to steal ideas ... err, I mean, share best practices with each other. Everyone benefits by hearing the creative thinking of each member of the group (particularly the rookies). Sharing plans is also a safety mechanism. If your plan is awful or you're embarking on a strategy that has failed in the past and is bound to fail again, others can stop you, or at least question your approach. That is valuable.

Some managers choose to have sales reps present their plans in private. That is fine too, and there's much benefit to an extended session where the manager and rep can ensure they're on the same page. One of the real keys to maximizing the impact from these plans is to review them on a regular basis. That is the easiest way to self-manage yourself, or for your sales manager to hold you accountable. All you need to do is pick up the plan and ask, "Am I doing what I said I needed to do in order to succeed?" It is truly that simple. Are you following the strategies you laid out in the plan? Are you tracking your activity against the metrics you said you would hit? Is your business plan driving what ends up on your calendar? There should be a lot of alignment between what we see in your plan and what we see on your calendar.

Preplanning Travel: Why Southwest Airlines is my Sales Force One

For many salespeople, air travel comes with the territory, literally. Over the past fifteen years, flying for business has become more and more challenging. Things were already on a downhill slide and then September 11, 2001, changed everything forever. The Transportation Safety Administration (TSA) has certainly added time, complexity, and inane policies to our travel routine. Makers of quart-size baggies had no idea how fashionable their product would become.

However, it is the airlines themselves that seem to have taken most of the joy and fun out of the once-friendly skies. Employees are sour, even bitter. And who can blame them? Many of them have lived through cut after cut in seniority, pay, and benefits. Leveraged buy-outs and bankruptcies destroyed pensions and retirement plans. On almost every airline, it's rare to encounter even one overtly happy, upbeat associate who is helping to make the travel experience more pleasurable. Beyond the unfriendly attitudes are the policies that are even more unfriendly to the salesperson.

As a fan of time-blocking, I encourage sales reps to not only block out time for prospecting, but also to prebook travel to cities where they're pursuing business. Airfares tend to be cheaper when purchased far in advance. But even more important than the savings, I want the sales rep committed to the trip. There is nothing that demonstrates commitment better than buying a ticket for a trip that's four or six weeks out *before* you have even scheduled one meeting with a prospect! If that doesn't cause you to time-block phone time to set up meetings, I don't know what will.

Unfortunately, almost every airline has resorted to charging usurious change fees. Here's a real story: Remember that client I fired

(Chapter 3)? Well, I had already purchased a $600 ticket for a trip that never materialized. When I called the airline to inquire about using the credit I had from canceling that trip, the agent on the phone was happy to inform me that I had another nine months to use that ticket, and he was even happier to let me know there would be a $150 fee to do so. Say what? You have been holding my money for months and want to charge me $150 to reschedule a trip. That policy may help a struggling company recoup some margin dollars, but in reality, it communicates to the customer that if you frequently change or cancel trips, you might want to consider using a more sales-friendly airline.

I'm an unabashed supporter of Southwest Airlines. Everything about Southwest is better: Its people. Its pricing. Its sales-friendly policies. When I was a salesperson, Southwest allowed me to business plan differently. I prebooked trips whenever possible, which allowed me to save money and fill more of my calendar with time out of the office. Southwest doesn't charge a penny to change a ticket. Because its fares were so low, I could easily bring a team member or two along for a second meeting with a prospect. For example, an opportunity would materialize with a prospect I had just met days earlier. The prospect would call and request another meeting to review a hot potential project. Since Southwest doesn't rip you off for last-minute purchases, I could confidently say to the prospect, "We can be there tomorrow or Friday. Which works better for you?" I would hang up the phone, jump onto the website at southwest.com, and less than sixty seconds later have two tickets purchased at a reasonable price for the senior account manager and myself.

Why do I love Southwest Airlines? Because Southwest is the sales airline! I'm convinced this airline has helped me do a lot more business than I otherwise would have. I even began seeking out prospective customers in cities Southwest served, and I encourage other salespeople to do the same. As I shifted more and more of my air travel to Southwest, I also began appreciating the culture of the company and the way its associates treated me. It is the only airline that makes me feel like a customer and a person, not a prisoner. As a salesperson, and now as a consultant, the mood I'm in when arriving at a client or prospect site matters. Southwest is part of my life and is like a partner in my business. The President of the United States has Air Force One. As a sales professional and sales coach, Southwest Airlines serves as my Sales Force One.

A Balanced Effort Produces a Balanced Pipeline

When it comes to executing the sales attack, not only do I like to talk about time blocking, but I also like to emphasize balance—in this case, balancing the sales effort across prospects and opportunities at various stages of the sales cycle. As much as anything else, this simple concept helps salespeople divide their time and their sales opportunities into clear segments.

Each business and salesperson uses different terminology to describe the stages of the sales cycle (or sales process). When it comes to managing your sales effort and time, for the sake of simplicity and clarity, I want you to divide your prospects and opportunities into just three categories: targeted, active, and hot.

1. *Targeted* accounts are those you are committed to proactively pursuing and moving to the Active stage.

2. *Active* accounts are those where you have started the sales dialogue, see potential opportunity for business, and need to continue working the process to move them to the Hot stage.

3. *Hot* is when real opportunities have emerged, there is some sense of urgency on your part, and you have either delivered a proposal or will do so very soon.

We would all agree these are reasonable categories. Sure, we could split hairs and parse out more segments with greater specificity to perfectly categorize every opportunity. My point here is not to project future business with great accuracy. The goal is for you to take in the big picture and get a handle on the health, status, and balance of your pipeline. Even more so, I want to provide a framework for segmenting your time to ensure you maintain a balanced pipeline of future business.

Why is this so important? Because no one defaults to prospecting mode. Experience shows that salespeople gravitate toward the hot opportunities in their pipeline. That's only natural and makes sense. Hot opportunities deserve our full attention so they remain hot. The danger begins when the salesperson obsesses over that segment of the pipeline at the expense of working the other segments. Chapter 2 describes how too many salespeople become "prisoners of hope" to the precious few hot deals they're attempting to close. And when we stop proactively working our active and targeted accounts, bad things happen in the future, particularly if we don't win as many of those hot opportunities as we "hoped" we would.

A healthy pipeline has three characteristics:

1. *It is full.* There are opportunities aplenty, and no one deal will make or break the quarter or the year.

2. *It shows movement.* Accounts and opportunities progress from one stage to the next; the majority of deals are not stale and growing mold.

3. *It is balanced.* When looking at the report we see accounts and opportunities in every segment.

A pipeline that's imbalanced in either direction is a sign of trouble ahead. If the vast majority of the accounts remain in the targeted stage, that's a sign we have either not put in a lot of effort starting new relationships or have done a poor job uncovering opportunities. When that's the case, the danger is that we have very few deals about to close and the short-term outlook for new sales is poor. A pipeline imbalanced in the other direction shows a good number of hot opportunities but very few in the active stage. While that portends well for short-term results, it's also a warning sign that we likely have not been working targeted accounts to open new active opportunities. We might be in good shape for now, but things look grim down the road if the active segment is not filled up.

There is no trick to maintaining a healthy pipeline that's full, showing movement, and balanced. It is completely a function of how we choose to invest our time. My cast-in-stone formula for helping salespeople maintain a healthy, balanced pipeline is simple: ⅓, ⅓, ⅓.

We must intentionally balance our time across each segment of the pipeline. Salespeople should spend a full third of their time working hot opportunities, another third working deals that are currently active, and the final third in proactive pursuit of targeted prospects that are not yet active.

It's that simple—⅓, ⅓, ⅓! Simple yet incredibly effective. I've had rep after rep tell me that following this one principle has been transformational for their new business efforts. Those who wholeheartedly attempt to segment their time in thirds come back with the same admission. They didn't have any clue how heavily they were overinvesting time with hot opportunities and how little time they were truly working to create new opportunities with targeted accounts.

Questions for Reflection

▶ For you to begin effectively blocking time for proactive prospecting, what type of systems or defenses might you need to put in place to protect yourself from interruptions?

▶ Do you have a handle on your sales math? What's the required activity level at the beginning of the sales process necessary to produce the amount of closed business you desire?

► Are your sales goals in writing? Have you articulated your strategies to develop new business and committed to certain key activity metrics?

► How will you hold yourself accountable to do what you say you need to?

► If your current pipeline of sales opportunities is not full, moving, and balanced, what can you begin doing immediately to restore it to health?

CHAPTER 15

Rants, Raves, and Reflections

We are approaching the conclusion of *New Sales. Simplified.* I want to thank you for investing in your development. I am honored you selected my first book to do it! I have several rants, raves, and reflections I'd now like to share with you that just didn't fit into the previous chapters, but belong in this book nonetheless.

Manners Matter

Receptionists, administrative assistants, and gatekeepers are people—people with feelings and often a good deal of influence. In the midst of all your craziness and hassle and intensity, try to keep that in mind.

It's not usually our first choice, but quite frequently we need to work through receptionists, gatekeepers, screeners, and assistants. Instead of being rude or frustrated with these people, befriend them. It won't always work. But it often does. A smile goes a long way, even over the phone. When you hear their other lines ringing off the hook in the background, demonstrate sensitivity and let them know it's fine to grab the other call and put you on hold. Use humor instead of anger. When you are stuck and frustrated about not getting calls returned, ask for help. People usually try to help other people. Ask what you may be doing wrong. Ask for advice. Be nice. You can be incredibly persistent and still be nice. And when you meet the receptionist or assistant in person (because I'm incredibly confident you will get the appointment you are seeking), spend a minute to visit with them. Make them feel appreciated and important. Making friends throughout the prospect's organization tends to help, not hurt, your sales effort.

Also, don't park next to your prospect's front door. Unless there's an overabundance of visitor parking spaces (which isn't likely), leave the prime spots out front for regular customers. Buyers and executives notice these things. You'll make a great last impression when your contact walks you to the door and sees you head to the back of the parking lot because you were considerate enough to leave the best spots open.

Attitude is Contagious

Your mom was right. Be careful whom you befriend. Salespeople love to bitch and complain. For many of us it's an art form. Don't get sucked into constant negative conversations. Stop hanging around with the perpetual whiners on the sales team. They aren't helping you achieve your goals or become the person you want to be.

Not long ago I was out in Las Vegas making sales calls with a CEO client. We stayed at Aria, a great new hotel. I went for dinner by myself and was seated next to two women who were obviously attending their company's national sales meeting. Their dinner conversation quickly ruined the excitement I had for an awesome Thai meal. The more tenured sales rep had nothing positive to say about her company, her sales support team, or her boss. Nada. She whined and complained about *everything* to the rookie rep. The timing was mind-blowing because I'd sketched the outline for this chapter on the flight just hours before I sat down to dinner. It took every bit of self-restraint I could muster not to lean over, apologize for eavesdropping, and tell the senior rep that she needed to resign if she felt the company was that bad, and to suggest that the rookie find better mentors if she wanted to succeed.

Please come to sales team meetings on time and with a smile on your face. I've done some coaching in a few companies where the vibe was not what it should be. I understand conditions may not be all rosy and that some sales cultures are not ideal. Regardless, your job is to bring your A-game every day. This is not accounting. We can't just show up and do our jobs well regardless of how miserable we are. Salespeople just going through the motions can't possibly operate at peak output. If it's that bad, find another job. Believe me, if you can sell, there are plenty of companies that would love to have you. If it isn't that bad, engage your heart and bring a winning attitude to the team and the rest of the company.

I've got one more thought about attitude. You do realize that the rest of the people in your company look to the sales organization to set the pace, to create hope about the future, and to deliver the results. Everyone is counting on us and looking to us. If we're down and pessimistic, the rest of the associates will follow our lead. The gal in the plant or the guy in accounts payable can't get the company more customers. You can! They are counting on you, and their livelihood depends on it. Take that responsibility seriously. And if your company has a prevailing anti-sales culture and very little respect for salespeople, then I can say emphatically that you work at the wrong place. Get out.

Your Appearance and Image Send a Message

Everybody has an opinion on fashion and what salespeople should wear. There's the professional dress camp committed to the suit and tie, regardless of whether you're in the corporate boardroom or setting up a new product display on a 100-degree day. On the other end of the spectrum, we have the "come as you are" promoters who don't mind being a few levels underdressed as long as you're being true to yourself.

My thinking is simple. We want to look fresh, successful, and confident. More important than the type of attire is paying attention to the condition and contemporary nature of what you're wearing. You notice how some out-of-date restaurants still have old-style tube televisions hanging in corners or by the bar? What looked great fifteen years ago looks absolutely dinosaurish today. When I see old TVs in a restaurant it causes me to question ownership's attention to detail and commitment to quality. I wonder how successful they are or if they might be cutting corners and buying lower-quality ingredients. All these thoughts come to mind simply because they haven't freshened the appearance of their establishment. You don't want potential customers wondering if you're successful or if you're cutting corners on quality. I am not saying you need to be hip, cool, and trendy. I certainly have never been described as any of those. But you need to look sharp.

A safe rule is to dress one level up from the customer. You can never go wrong being slightly overdressed. Don't cheap out on shoes and your carrying bag. Cheap shoes look cheap. Cheap vinyl bags look like cheap vinyl bags. Nice shoes make you feel like a million bucks. Keep them clean and polished. People notice. And I have one special request: Please lose the embroidered company logo shirt. Everything about it is wrong. There is no way to send the message we want to send wearing an oversize logo on our chest. We are sales professionals and we don't wear uniforms. Next time you are in an airport, with a critical eye, take note of the myriad of folks wearing logo shirts. Ask yourself if any of them look in style. The other problem with the logo is that it screams, "We are all about us! Our company is great!"

Go After the Giant Competitor and Play to Win

Stop fearing the giant competitor. I see too many sales reps with defeatist attitudes when it comes to going head-to-head against a massive competitor. They're ready to throw in the towel before the fight even begins.

Bigger is not always better. Bigger is bigger. Sometimes bigger is harder. It certainly is often slower, clumsier, inflexible, arrogant, and complacent. I like to compete against slow, clumsy, inflexible, arrogant, and complacent companies and you should, too.

Keep in mind that in most cases you are not competing against the entire organization. You're competing against the giant's sales guy or sales gal and a small team. That changes the perspective, doesn't it? Are you more committed to winning than they are? Will you go the extra mile to build deep relationships, to do better discovery work, to bring fresher ideas and more value, to better tailor your presentation and solution to the customer's needs?

Last year I was preparing some coaching content for a very small company that regularly competed with the industry giant. I read an article that reviewed historic David versus Goliath military and business battles. The data showed that the "Goliath" won between 70 percent and 80 percent of the battles while the "David" was victorious 20 percent to 30 percent of the time. While the Goliath's record is indeed impressive, there is also a bright spot for the smaller competitor. How would you feel if you knew beforehand that you would compete with the biggest, baddest competitor on the planet ten times over the next year and would walk away with two or three huge victories for yourself and your business? I get kind of excited thinking about reaping the spoils from those few victories. That may certainly make it worth the ten battles, even if we got our butts handed to us the other seven or eight times.

Winners Get in the Office Early and in the Deal Early

It concerns me when I am on-site at a client's office bright and early, but don't see salespeople hitting it hard. Early morning is not for catching up with coworkers, news headlines, or e-mail. Winners arrive early and tackle their highest-priority items first thing in the morning.

They set the pace for their entire day by taking control right from the outset.

It drives me crazy when salespeople meander into the office late—unless, of course, they're out making sales calls. Even worse is the salesperson who starts the day reading and responding to e-mails, most of which have nothing to do with proactive selling or developing new business. Without even realizing it, these reps spend the first third of the day in a completely reactive mode responding to whatever comes their way. They may be busy, but they certainly are not productive.

Top-performing salespeople are not only in the office early, they also find their way into deals early. True sales hunters work their target accounts prior to opportunities materializing. They're out in front of the curve, building relationships, penetrating the accounts, launching their sales weapons, turning over rocks, and attempting to unearth opportunities. When something concrete emerges, they are on the front end and positioned perfectly to help lead the prospect. In contrast, most reactive salespeople are either too busy playing account manager to work their target list or are not assertive enough to discover opportunities early in the process. Instead, they follow, rather than lead, the prospect, and they usually end up playing their competitor's already-in-progress game.

If you want to win at new business development, get to the office early. Own the morning. Tackle high-payoff activities first. Work your strategic target account list. Ignore the voices telling you not to call on accounts unless they're perfectly qualified, just like you should ignore the liars telling you that proactive prospecting doesn't work anymore. Get in front of your target prospects. Make friends, penetrate the account, figure out how your potential customer does business. Help the prospect see pains, problems, and issues that you can address. Put yourself in "Position A" so that when these prospects are ready to look for solutions, you're the natural first choice. Then enjoy watching your lazy, reactive, overqualifying competitors play catch-up while eating your dust.

Take Real Vacations and Stay Off the Grid

Vacations are critical for high-performance people. I don't need to tell you how overconnected you are. We used to feel bad for those poor souls who carried beepers around. They were always on call and tethered to their jobs in case of a crisis. Ha! Today we thumb-scroll through business e-mails during dinner with our families and don't give it a second thought. Our best customers text-message us after hours with questions or requests. Most of us in sales are operating at a pace that's hard to sustain.

Vacations are not just for selfish time or to enjoy the family (although those are great reasons to get away). Real vacations make us better at our jobs. Vacations refresh and recharge us. Even more essential, they provide time away from the grind, allowing our minds to go into hyperdrive attacking issues we simply cannot get to when we are connected all the time. That's why it is so important to truly unplug (which sounds silly, since all of our communication devices are now wireless). Checking and responding to e-mail a few times a day destroys the value of vacation. It not only sends the wrong message to the people you're vacationing with, but it puts your brain right back in work mode. You end up cheating yourself. Instead of allowing your mind the space, clarity, and creativity that comes from being away, you end up working on the same old junk you always do. What a waste. I promise that you are actually hurting your work by working while on vacation. Chew on that theory for a few minutes.

I worked ridiculously hard my first year back in full-time consulting. I had to. But I also managed to take several vacations because I needed to. Said differently, my business needed me to take vacation so that I could return with better ideas and fully charged batteries. On two trips I completely unplugged. So much so that I changed my voice mail greeting and e-mail auto-reply to inform people that I was "off the grid" and unable to receive messages until I returned to work. It was unbelievable how much work my brain did while unplugged from day-to-day business. I read a book by the brilliant

Alan Weiss that hit the spot for me. I outlined the table of contents for the book you're reading right now. I caught up on several months of *Entrepreneur* magazine. And I got all kinds of new ideas for my business while sitting on the beach in Central America. My wife never once felt cheated because I wasn't on the phone and I stayed away from e-mail. And not one client was upset with me. In fact, quite the opposite, they were pleased that I got away and appreciated how fired up I was when I came back. Take real vacations. They make you better at what you do.

Team Selling: Make the Most of Your Resources

Way back in college, one of the biggest lessons I took away from pledging the business fraternity Delta Sigma Pi was to *use my resources*. The fraternity brothers would give the pledge class what appeared to be insurmountable assignments. When a pledge would express frustration or complain, the brothers would simply offer their standard reply: Use your resources! It was incredible training for the business world.

Too many salespeople operate as mavericks and lone rangers. They attempt to tackle every situation with prospective customers on their own. It could be out of ignorance, pride, or pigheadedness. Whatever the case, it hurts them.

Individually, we don't have all the answers and we aren't always the best suited to handle sales situations with prospects and customers. Learn to use your resources. Who can help you move a particular opportunity forward? Is it someone in your network who has a relationship with your targeted account? What options do you have when every time you contact a prospective customer you run up against a certain important player who doesn't respect or even like you? It will happen, and we should be prepared.

I had a lot of success team selling. I loved bringing others from my company along on important sales calls. And why not? As long as my guests (including chief executives) were willing to let me structure and control the call, I welcomed all the help I could get.

It's important that we know in which areas we are strong when it comes to selling, but just as critical to be aware of our blind spots and shortfalls. If there are certain types of buyers that you regularly have trouble connecting with, recruit appropriate help from your company. If a highly technical buyer tends to dismiss you as the big-talking, nontechnical salesperson, then bring your own technical genius along to connect with the buyer's own experts. I've seen magic happen by using other resources when I was getting nowhere fast on my own. My super-techie guy shows up and the buyer pretends I'm not even in the room. The two of them go back and forth speaking in code not intended to be deciphered by sales guys. It's awesome.

When you're stuck—or even better, before you get stuck—review your resource options. You don't need to go it alone. There is no extra credit for trying to be a hero flying solo. Get help and maximize your chances of winning.

Beware Who Is Telling You Not to Prospect

There are plenty of loud voices out there who want you to believe prospecting doesn't work anymore. My warning is to be very careful who you listen to. Experience shows that the very same salespeople urging you not to proactively prospect for new business are the ones who don't do it themselves. These failing reps boldly declare that calling on prospects who are not already pursuing you is a waste of time.

Here is the truth: Those proclaiming that prospecting is not an effective method for developing new business are doing so out of ignorance and with false motives. Ask the next person who tries to dissuade you how much personal experience he has prospecting. Ask these naysayers when they, in fact, "tried" it for themselves and for how long. Ask if they had a strategically selected, finite, focused list of target prospects. Ask what type of weapons they developed for their sales attack. Ask them to share the sales story they used to get a prospect's attention. Then look them straight in the eye and ask flat out how many times they picked up the phone attempting to connect with target accounts on their list. Trust me, they won't appreciate the inquisition because their answers are lame.

I worked with a client that had lots of family members in the business. Probably too many. A brother on the sales team lived in one city while the sister who also sold lived in another. They were both remote sales offices, with headquarters and the production operation located in a third city. The sister was a sales rock star. The brother, not so much. The brother told anyone who would listen that cold-calling did not work. The sister was a proactive calling machine. Every month the brother would have his excuses why his business was not what it should be. The sister would report in sharing recent success stories from her telephone and face-to-face prospecting. In spite of the sister's success, the brother maintained his stance that prospecting didn't work. Two people, same upbringing, same amount of experience, with very different perspectives and very different results. Let's be real, people. The brother did not want to prospect. And just like so many false sales teachers today, he doesn't want you to prospect, either.

Be careful who you listen to. I've sold millions and millions of dollars by prospecting for new business. I can take you to any number of cities and point to the buildings of companies whose business I personally acquired because I proactively selected and pursued the prospect.

CHAPTER 16

New Business Development Selling Is Not Complicated

If you picked up this book believing that prospecting and new business development were shrouded in some sort of mystery, I hope that I've debunked that myth for you. There's no great mystery, and those who are most successful keep it incredibly simple.

Proactively pursuing new business is not complicated. Prospective customers have needs. We have potential solutions for those needs. When charged with developing new business from new accounts, our job is to engage with potential customers to determine if what we sell aligns with what these prospects need. It's that simple.

New customers are the lifeblood of most businesses. If there were a continuous steady stream of warm leads pouring into sales organizations, salespeople would thrive by just reacting and responding to this abundant supply of inbound demand. But in 100 percent of the businesses I have seen, that simply is not the case. To grow sales and acquire new accounts, we must become successful at prospecting and developing new business.

There is No Magic Bullet

I love meeting new salespeople or kicking off a relationship with a new client's sales team. Usually, salespeople are thankful for a sympathetic ear, and most of them are looking forward to getting some help. There is often a sense of excitement that someone from the outside has arrived to share some new tricks. It doesn't take long before the questions start flowing my way:

➤ "What's the most powerful closing technique guaranteed to work every time?"

➤ "Can you help us with selling to committees comprised of more women than men?"

➤ "When the prospect is scheduling three competitors for presentations, is it best to go first or last? Does it make a difference if the presentations are on a Friday?"

➤ "What's your secret sauce for...?"

You're smiling, but those are sincere questions that salespeople want answers to. My standard reply is that these are all interesting questions that we may get to, at some point (not likely). But I've got my own questions that are probably a more helpful place for us to start:

➤ I'd like you to show me your actual prospect lists. Pull them up or print me a copy of your specific list of target accounts. Can you please tell me the strategic thinking that led to creating these lists?

➤ Now tell me about your account focus. How much time and effort have you invested working that list?

➤ Let me hear your sales story. What are you saying to prospects about what you do? How do you talk about your business?

➤ Let's talk about the phone. How much time are you spending proactively calling prospects? How's that working for you?

- ► Outline for me your structure for meeting with a prospect. How do you conduct sales calls?

- ► How much of your time is spent managing existing customers or responding to service issues, as compared with the amount of time you're dedicating to proactive selling?

- ► Grab your pipeline report. Can you please tell me about the volume of opportunities you're working and how you are investing time across deals in various stages of the sales cycle?

- ► You've got a written business plan, right? Pull it out. What are your strategies for opening new accounts and what key sales activities have you committed to?

The resulting discomfort from my blunt questions speaks volumes as to why so many salespeople underperform when it comes to developing new business. They want help running trick plays but are not interested in the basics, like blocking and tackling. The truth is that there are no secret sales moves. There is no magic bullet. As badly as we all want one, it does not exist.

New Sales Success Results from Executing the Basics Well

Chapter 4 laid out the basic framework for a successful new business sales attack. As you wrap up your time with this book, I strongly encourage you to revisit the New Sales Driver framework and work to nail it cold:

THE NEW SALES DRIVER

    A. Select *targets.*

    B. Create and deploy *weapons.*

    C. Plan and execute the *attack.*

It all starts with targets (Chapter 5). This is the first step because it is impossible to launch a new business development effort without knowing who we're going to attack. A well-chosen, finite, focused, written, and workable list is essential and allows us to shift our attention to the weapons we will be firing at these targets.

When headed into battle, it really helps to have powerful weapons (Chapters 6 and 7). Not only do we need these weapons within reach, but we must be proficient at firing them! No weapon is more critical or more frequently deployed than our sales story. Nothing will increase your personal sales effectiveness more than sharpening your story. I challenge you to review Chapter 8 and make the effort to run through the sales story exercise to draft your own power statement. Having a compelling, differentiating, client-focused story will increase your confidence and empower you to engage prospects.

It's also critical to master the proactive phone call and face-to-face sales call (Chapters 9 through 11). Sound fundamentals early in the sales process dramatically improve your chances of winning down the road. Too many salespeople gloss over these mundane elements of prospecting, preferring to focus on the more glamorous aspects like delivering their presentation.

And while on the topic of my (least) favorite word, please remember that discovery must always precede presentation. By sales law, a first meeting shall never be a presentation, and nowhere is it written that presentations must be monologues. Dare to be different and break out of the mold. Be more like Jerry, the kitchen guy who cut a hole in my wall without permission, and less like Frank, who bored the boardroom with pictures of his company's buildings, client logos, and business processes.

Above all else, you've got to take control of your calendar so that you're in a position to plan and execute the new business attack (Chapter 14). Powerful weapons and strategic targets mean nothing if you don't fly the mission. Articulate your sales plan and commit to the necessary level of proactive new business development activity. Sales is a verb, at least in this book. Get into action and execute a high-frequency attack. Beware of the gravitational pull of account management and customer service. Stop playing good corporate citizen and selfishly guard your selling time. Block off chunks in your calendar for prospecting, and treat those blocks of time as if they're as important as a meeting with a CEO.

Finally, keep in mind that buyers instinctively resist salespeople. We must sell against that reality on a daily basis. Run every aspect of selling through the filter that forces you to ask how the buyer will perceive you. Your approach, voice tone, word choices, and method for conducting phone and face-to-face sales calls—all contribute to whether buyers will raise or lower their sales defensive shields.

Thank you for reading. I sincerely wish you the best of success in your pursuit of new customers. You can keep up with me on Twitter @mike_weinberg or on my blog: newsalescoach.com.

Now go forth and sell.

INDEX

Abraham, Danny, 85, 130, 131
ACBJ (American Cities Business
    Journals), 60
accountability, 191
accounts
    active, 194
    "babysitting" of, 20–21
    hot, 194, 195
    risky, 57
    segmenting of, 55–57
    targeted, 194, *see also* target
    account selection
    types of, 194
action, 181–182, 190
active accounts, 194
administrative assistants, 199–200
agenda, sharing your, 136–138
airline industry, 192
American Cities Business Journals
    (ACBJ), 60
analytical people, 26
anger, 123
appearance, 201–202

attack, *see* sales attack
attitude, 200–201

balanced pipeline, 194–196
bankers, 59
Bank of America, 47
base compensation, 37
best practices, 11
blogs, 24–25, 70
Book of Lists, 53, 60
brainstorming, 98–99
    business books, 25
    business plans, 188–192
    buyer's process, 127–128
    buyer's resistance, 153–161, 213
    across industries, 154
    preventing and minimizing,
        157–161
    and shaping customer perception,
        156–157
    and stereotypes of salespeople,
        154–155

calendars, 23–24, 183, 212–213
case studies, 71
clarity, 31
clients (customers)
  asking for help from, 99–100
  identifying style of, 134–136
  needs of, 1, 138
  resistance from, *see* buyer's
    resistance
  in sales story, 77–80, 87–91, 99
  shaping perceptions of, 156–157
closings, 62
clothing, 202
coaching, 30–31
cold calling, 6–7, 19–20, *see also*
    proactive telephone calls; sales
    calls
commissions, 38
commodity businesses, 103–105
companies, 29–41
consulting at, 30–31
  flawed compensation plans of,
    36–38
  hunter-farm sales role in, 34–36
  mistreatment of sales departments
    in, 38–41
  strategies of, 31–32
  views of sales departments in,
    32–34
compensation plans, 36–38
competitors, 202–203
confidence
  for phone prospecting, 18
  with sales story, 76, 82–83
construction companies, 59
consulting, 30–31
corporate citizens, 21–22
credibility, 141
customer relationship management
  (CRM), 9
customers, *see* clients

default
  to the buyer's process, 127–128
  to prospecting mode, 182–183
demos, 45, 71

dialogues, monologues vs., 128–131
differentiation, 81–82, 176–179, 212
differentiators, 87, 91–92, 136
digital marketing tools, 70
directional questions, 142–143
distractions, 17–18
dot-com bubble, 6
dream targets, 62–63
Dun & Bradstreet, 60–61

economic prosperity, 5–6
elevator pitch, 89
e-mail, 69
emotional quotient (EQ), 19
entertainment, 72
existing accounts
  "babysitting" of, 20–21
  segmenting of, 55–57
existing clients, asking for help from,
  99–100
expertise, 70, 72, 88

face-to-face sales call, 70, 125–132
  avoiding default to buyer's process
    in, 127–128
  dialogue vs. monologue in,
    128–131
  importance of mastering, 212
  plans for, 125–127
  selling from same side of table in,
    131–132
facility tours, 71
failure, *see* new business development
  failure
financial crisis of late 2000s, 6
finite lists, 53
fit, 120, 148–149
fixed compensation, 37
flooring sales representatives, 59
focus, 15–16
focused lists, 54

gatekeepers, 199–200
goals, 188–189

growth
  as factor in account segmentation, 57
  lack of, 24–25
  guilt, 122

headline (power statement), 90
High-Profit Selling (Mark Hunter), 82
Holmes, Chet, 62
honesty, 12
Hoover's, 60–61
hope, 14
hot accounts, 194, 195
humor, 122, 199–200
Hunter, Mark, 82
hunter-farm sales role, 34–36

Iannarino, Anthony, 62
image, 201–202
inbound marketing, 108
indirect selling, 59–60
individual business plans, 188–192
industry associations, 61
inside reps, 56, 118
intentional imbalance, 57

knowledge, 12–13
Konrath, Jill, 25, 86

large customers, 57
Lasorda, Tommy, 130
learning, 24–25
likability, 18–19, 22
LinkedIn, 61
loan officers, 59
local business journals, 60

manners, 199–200
marketing
  inbound, 108
  materials for, 69–70, 100

with telemarketing, 109, *see also* proactive telephone calls
math, 186–188
meetings, 113, 119, 171–172, *see also* face-to-face sales call
mentors, 8–10
metrics, 188, 190
"Mirroring," 135
mission, company, 31
monologues, dialogues vs., 128–131
morning, working in, 203–204

negative attitudes, 17
networking, 69
new business development, 209–211
  challenges with, 182
  commitment to, 183
  creating dialogue for, 129
  framework for, 47–50
  and sales compensation, 37–38
  time blocking for, 183–184
new business development failure, *xiii*, 11–27
  and calendars, 23–24
  and existing accounts, 20–21
  and good corporate citizens, 21–22
  and hope, 14
  inability to tell sales story in, 14–15
  lack of knowledge in, 12–13
  lack of learning and growth in, 24–25
  and likability, 18–19, 22
  missed opportunities in, 16
  negative attitudes and pessimism in, 17
  phone mistakes in, 17–20
  role of personality in, 25–26
  role of waiting in, 13
  sales process ownership in, 22–23
  target account selection in, 15–16
New Sales Driver, 47–48, 211–212, *see also* sales attack; sales weapons; target account selection
niceness, 21–22
Northwestern Mutual, 44

objections, 148–149
obstacles, 190
offerings, 87, 91, 101
opportunity-seeking questions, 143–144
overqualifying, 113

patience, 13
perceptions, shaping, 156–157
personal development, 190–191
personality, 25–26
personal questions, 142
pessimism, 17
phone prospecting
    importance of, 69
    mistakes made with, 17–20
    see also proactive telephone calls
physical appearance, 201–202
pipeline, balanced, 194–196
pitches, 174, see also presentations
planning
    for face-to-face sales calls, 125–127
    with individual business plans, 188–192
    of travel, 192–194
    see also sales attack
podcasts, 70
PowerPoint presentations, 128, 164, 170–171, see also presentations
power statements
    in proactive telephone calls, 116–117
    in sales calls, 139–141
    in sales story, 89–98, 102–103
premium pricing, 81–82
presentations, 163–179
    differentiation with, 176–179, 212
    expectations of, 72
    failure with, 22–23
    meetings before, 171–172
    problems with, 163–169
    as sales term, 45
    selling vs., 128, 176
    success with, 170–171
    without meetings beforehand, 173–176

pricing, premium, 81–82
pride, 82–83
printed marketing materials, 69–70
"prisoners of hope," 14, 63
proactive behavior, 13, 113
proactive telephone calls, 107–123
    asking for meetings during, 113, 119
    building bridges with, 118
    fresh starts with, 108–109
    importance of mastering, 212
    introductory phrases for, 113–116
    and leaving voicemails, 121–123
    magic words for, 120
    mindset for, 109
    mini power statements for, 116–117
    purpose of, 112
    scripts vs. no scripts for, 111–112
    voice tone and approach for, 109–111
    see also sales calls
probing questions, 70–71
problem solving, 20, 145
proposals
    early, 23
    requests for, 16, 72
    types of, 72
prospecting
    defaulting to, 182–183
    fear of, 5
    people warning against, 207–208
    projected death of, 6–8
    struggles with, 5–6
public speaking, 107
puffery, 80–81
punctuality, 203–204

questions, 141–148, 156–157
quotas, 21

rapport, 19, 134–136
real estate bubble, 6
receptionists, 199–200
references, case study, 72–73
referrals, 59–60

Reilly, Tom, 14
requests for proposals (RFPs), 16, 72
research, 142–143
resistance, from buyer, *see* buyer's
    resistance
Revson, Charles, on selling, 80
RFPs (requests for proposals), 16, 72
risky accounts, 57

sales
    simplicity of, 1
    as verb, 48, 212
Sales 2.0, 6–8
sales attack, 47, 48, 181–196
    and a balanced pipeline, 194–196
    and business plans, 188–192
    and defaulting to prospecting
        mode, 182–183
    and sales as a numbers game,
        186–188
    and time blocking, 183–184
    and travel preplanning, 192–194
sales calls, 133–151
    asking probing questions in,
        141–148
    building rapport in, 134–136
    cleaning up client issues in, 138
    defining and scheduling next step
        in, 149–151
    determining fit and seeking
        objections in, 148–149
    importance of structuring,
        133–134
    phases of, 134
    power statements in, 139–141
    selling portion of, 147–148
    sharing the agenda for, 136–138
    see also cold calling; face-to-face
        sales call; proactive telephone
        calls
sales cycle, 194
sales departments
    mistreatment of, 38–41
    views of, 32–34
Salesforce.com, 10
sales managers, 8, 32–34
sales mentors, 8–10

salespeople, stereotypes of, 154–155
sales process, 22–23
sales process questions, 144–147
sales story, 14–15, 75–105
    building blocks of, 87
    client issues in, 87–91, 99
    for commodity businesses,
        103–105
    differentiation and pricing in,
        81–82
    effective, 85
    exercise for drafting, 98–101
    focus on client in, 77–80
    importance of, 68–69
    ineffective, 76–77
    power statement in, 89–98,
        102–103
    producing confidence and pride
        with, 76, 82–83
    "so what?" test for, 86
    telling of, 80–81
sales weapons, 47, 48
    importance of, 67, 212
    presentations as, 170
    types of, 68–73
    see also face-to-face sales call;
        proactive telephone calls; sales
        story
sameness, 81
samples, 71
scripts, 111–112
segmenting, of accounts, 55–57
Seinfeld, Jerry, on holding reserva-
    tions, 185
selecting targets, *see* target account
    selection
seller-buyer relationship, 131
selling
    indirect, 59–60
    presentations vs., 128, 176
    in sales calls, 147–148
    from the same side of table,
        131–132
    team, 71–72, 206–207
senior leadership, 52
September 11th terrorist attacks, 6
simple sales model, 2–5
Slim-Fast, 32

SMEs (subject matter experts), 72
SNAP Selling (Jill Konrath), 25, 86
social media
  effectiveness of, 108
  importance of, 69
  potential of, 7–8
Southwest Airlines, 4–5, 192–194
"so what?" test (sales stories), 86
specific-issue questions, 143–144
stereotypes of salespeople, 154–155
storytelling, 80–81, *see also* sales story
strategic questions, 142–143
strategies
  in business plans, 189–190
  of companies, 31–32
  in target account selection, 52–53
subject matter experts (SMEs), 72

Target, 130
target account selection, 15–16,
    51–66, 211–212
  characteristics of target list in,
    53–55
  dream targets in, 62–63
  in New Sales Driver model, 47, 48
  preparing for, 57–59
  referrals and indirect selling for,
    59–60
  resources for, 60–62
  and segmenting accounts, 55–57
  strategy in, 52–53
  time spent on, 34
  types of targets in, 63–65
targeted accounts, 194
team selling, 71–72, 206–207
telemarketing, 109, *see also* proactive
    telephone calls
TheSalesBlog.com, 62
time blocking, 183–184, 213
time management, 23–24

tone of voice, 109–111, 158
trade shows, 61, 71
transitional phrase (power statement),
    90
transparency, 12
Transportation Safety Administration
    (TSA), 192
travel, 192–194
Twitter, 8, 24

Unilever, 131

vacations, 205–206
value, 120
Value-Added Selling (Tom Reilly), 14
value proposition, 89
victim mentality, 17
videos, 70
"visit" (magic word), 120
voice, tone of, 109–111, 158
voice mail, 69, 121–123

waiting, 13, 45
Wal-Mart, 130
warm leads, 13
weapons, *see* sales weapons
webinars, 70
Weinberg, Mike, *xiii*
Weiss, Alan, 40, 206
white papers, 70
workable lists, 55
working hours, 203–204
written lists, 54–55

YouTube, 70